MW01226154

# FOR THE GOOD OF ALL, NOW!

## DAVID CURRIE

10-10-10
Publishing

Publisher
10-10-10 Publishing
Markham, ON
Canada

Printed in Canada and the United States of America

# DEDICATION

To my Grandchildren
Curtis, Taylor, and Natalie

# TABLE OF CONTENTS

# FOREWORD

You may feel like the daily news is full of depressing problems that seem too big for you to overcome. You tolerate behavior in adults that you would find abhorrent in your children. The resulting hopelessness has a paralyzing effect, making it seem as though change for the better is out of reach. *For the Good of All, NOW!* challenges that hopelessness, by inviting you to resurrect the timeless connection you have with others, and with our planet, through the power of self, the power of community, and the power of connection.

In each chapter of *For the Good of All, NOW!*, David dives into how you can build connections that can accomplish significant change for your family, your community, and your world. What David describes is nothing new. Yet, through his powerful and inspiring narrative, David explores how you can embrace your history of oneness to shape your present and future. You will learn how to build community in a way that steps outside of the current political structure by working at the local level to create meaningful change.

*For the Good of All, NOW!* is not just another guide that addresses one problem or challenge. Instead, this book is a guide to understanding how you can thrive as a member of the human race, not just as an individual. David demonstrates how you can embrace Power With, instead of Power Over. Dust off your hope for the world and get inspired as David shares how you can contribute and connect, For the Good of All, NOW!

Raymond Aaron
*New York Times* Bestselling Author

# PREAMBLE

**W**e live in tumultuous times. How is it possible that today, humans, the stars of the natural kingdom, have strayed off course so radically that we now face the threat of self-extinction? The answers to this question lie in understanding how we got here, why we do what we do, and what we need to do now to adapt and achieve a more glorious future.

Coming to terms with these questions is uncomfortable and necessary. It is uncomfortable because the questions challenge our assumptions about living on Earth; and the greater the challenge, the greater the tendency to avoid the discomfort. The result is apathy, a lack of self-belief, and even resistance to confront reality. We are preconditioned to revert to the norm even if the norm results in tragedy. But that doesn't mean we can't change our conditioning and create a new normal, even as we face challenges on multiple fronts.

*For the Good of All, NOW!* is a simple guidebook to navigate the complex world we live in. I suggest that, despite the enormity of the challenges ahead, we are capable of living up to the potential of being our 'better selves,' because we are gifted with the ability to understand the implications of our actions and the imagination to set a new course. Since the dawn of our existence, we have risen to such daunting challenges three times. We can do it a fourth time.

It is possible to foresee a more glorious future by understanding our past, and I will describe both what brings us here and where we are headed. Although the necessary shift is immense, the path is simple if you have a good map and good company. Reconnecting deeply with all life is natural. It is life-changing for those who choose this path. But this does not necessarily lead to change.

Change only happens when *you* are self-empowered to make the conscious choice to make change happen. This book will show you why and how to become self-empowered because, if *you* don't choose change, no one else will.

# Our Lady of Unity & Peace
## (*SAYÉDOT ALWÉHDAH WASSALAM*)

In 1983, during the Lebanese Civil War, attached to the U.S. Embassy was a young Lebanese soldier, Adib Rouhana, who was wounded while successfully defending against an attack on the escort of a diplomat on his way to the airport. His valor and the injury he sustained earned him the opportunity to come to the United States. But I get ahead of myself. This is a true story of how, when heart and spirit manifest in the world as compassion, the ripples create ripples of their own, in ever-widening circles.

A long time ago, the small village of Ammiq was built by hand, using the plentiful stones on an ancient mountainside above the fertile Bekaa valley in Lebanon. Small houses with a couple of rooms and dirt or stone floors. No running water or electricity. By the 1950s, when this story begins, there were 100 homes and two houses of worship, one for the Catholics and the other for the Lebanese Maronites, an ethnic-religious group founded by a Syrian hermit in the late 4th century.

One household in Ammiq stood out as a central gathering place. This was the house of the tenant farmer Mikhael Rouhana and his wife Adla and their family. This is the house where my friend Adib spent his early years with his parents and five brothers and two sisters.

Life as a tenant farmer, cultivating 400 acres of vegetables to be sold by wholesalers in the markets of Beirut, produced enough money to pay the lease to the wealthy valley landowner. There was never any money left over. But, then again, no one in Ammiq had any money to speak of. The Rouhana family house had always been the center of the community's social life. A home warmed by good company with poetry, song, dance, conversation, and laughter. Mikhael would sing poems, often making them up as he went. Adib would play the derbakki—a goblet shaped drum—and the shepherds would play their flutes.

Every year at harvest time itinerant Bedouins and Gypsies would arrive to work the lush fields. Mikhael would set up tents and make sure to feed them. One year a nursing mother and child, both starving, came to Ammiq with the migrant workers. That evening, Adla prepared a big bowl of bulgur porridge for dinner and Mikhael invited the mother and child to eat with the family. They urged their children and the guests to eat to their content, as they had already eaten.

Later that night, Adib was awakened by a clinking sound. He got up and parted the curtains that served as doors to peek in his parents' bedroom. Even as Adib describes the scene fifty or more years later, tears come to his eyes. There sat his parents stirring spoonfuls of sugar from the rations they got from the United Nations into a bowl of hot water to feed themselves. He cried as he knew full well that they had not eaten.

An earthquake in the late 1950s damaged the old stone buildings in the village and the United Nations provided funds to rebuild new homes made of cement, but no one knew how to build houses with cement. Anyway, even getting the cement up to the village would be impractical.

Around the world, the young leave their rural homes and become part of a huge diaspora seeking opportunity in the wider world. One of these emigrants was a nephew of Mikhael's living in Germany, where he worked as an urban planning architect. Mikhael wrote to him for advice and got much more than he had asked for.

The nephew designed a whole new village down in the valley with a road, electricity, and all the little houses laid out for every family. The old stone buildings, including the churches, were left up on the mountainside and some are still standing to this day. But there was no funding to build new churches.

Mikhael went to the elders to present the challenge: there was no money to build one house of worship, let alone two. He proposed that perhaps, if he raised the funds, they could build one and share it. The elders were decidedly unimpressed—"Who is going to worship in the other man's church? No one has ever done such a thing. Besides, where would the money come from to build it? This is like trying to make a river flow uphill."

So, Mikhael, who knew all the children who had moved away, wrote to tell them of his plan and to ask for their help. Soon enough, money started coming in from the scattered sons and daughters of Ammiq. Mikhael went back to the elders: "Look, the money is coming in." Still, the elders were skeptical about the project, but they didn't say no. Mikhael then took it upon himself to write to the Pope to ask him for a donation.

He described the situation and told the Pope of his plan to build a house of worship called Our Lady of Unity and Peace, as such a name would be acceptable to the Catholics, the Maronites and the Eastern Orthodox. All the faiths would practice in a shared church. So impressed was the Pope with this extraordinary plan that soon enough a letter arrived from Rome and enclosed was a donation of $5,000! This, in addition to all the other donations, was enough to build a big church.

As Ammiq was the only village with such a church for miles around, nearby villagers would come to worship there too. It became apparent that there was nowhere to celebrate the important life events that bring people together: birth, marriage, death. So, the ever-resourceful Mikhael raised funds to build a hall alongside the church. It was the only such hall in the surrounding area. People came and celebrated. When they came, the women of Ammiq, despite their own meager circumstances, would always cook and prepare food for the guests. Born of generosity, the spirit of *Our Lady of Peace and Unity* radiates generosity. It is clear that even ancient and passionately held customs can dissolve, like sugar in warm water, when compassion arises.

It will not surprise you to know that the father's spirit lives on in the son Adib, the most generous person I have ever met.

May the spirit of Mikhael Rouhana and the spirit of Unity and Peace be with us.

# CHAPTER 1

# DEEP SELF

### "Of The Empire" by Mary Oliver

We will be known as a culture that feared death
and adored power, that tried to vanquish insecurity
for the few and cared little for the penury of the many.
We will be known as a culture that taught
and rewarded the amassing of things, that spoke
little if at all about the quality of life for
people (other people), for dogs, for rivers.
All the world, in our eyes, they will say, was a commodity.
And they will say that this structure
was held together politically, which it was, and
they will say also that our politics was no more
than an apparatus to accommodate the feelings of
the heart, and that the heart, in those days,
was small, and hard, and full of meanness.

From *Red Bird*—Poems by Mary Oliver, 2008 p.46

The reason I am writing this book is because it is easier to imagine the annihilation of billions of people as a result of "Man's inhumanity to man" (Robert Burns, 1784) than to imagine achieving unity and peace on Earth. If this statement is as dispiriting to you as it is to me, then you will understand the purpose for writing the book.

The true story of "Our Lady of Unity & Peace" and Mary Oliver's poem "Of The Empire" paint two very different pictures. This guidebook will also paint two very different pictures and two very different outcomes. If you want to live in unity and peace, I invite you to join me as I explain how it can and will, finally, be accomplished. My goals are: 1) To give you as many tools as I can to allow you to attract more happiness and serenity in your life than *you* ever imagined, now; 2) To provide an opportunity for humanity to coalesce around the ancient and new technologies presented here; and, 3) To assemble a worldwide grassroots movement resulting in a human society that is laser-focused on the wellbeing of the planet: For the Good of All, NOW!

Although the topic could fill a library, I want as many people as possible to engage. Please don't expect a scholarly dissertation this is not a monograph. I am hoping to hit a Goldilocks happy medium: not too hard, not too soft, just right. There are no sweeping inspirational passages nor cliff-hanging dramatic plots in this book. Rather it contains practical wisdom, some science and history, and innovative strategies using time-tested methods. It won't dig as deeply as some would like, and it will be too much for others. It should be read while keeping the Resources section of the website handy: www.forthgoodofallnow.org. In all these respects, I think of it as a self-empowerment manual for the transition we are in.

The two main thrusts are self-empowerment, based on Thich Nhat Hahn's *The Art of Power,* and the why, what, when and how related to a local-to-global movement: For the Good of All, NOW! The first three chapters will follow a pattern: Who, Where, How, and What. Section A asks Who am I? or Who are we? Section B asks Where am I—or we— going? Section C: How am I—or we—getting there? Section D: What changes can I—or we—expect to experience? Section E: provides a brief summary of the chapter or suggests additional resources. Between the website (www.forthegoodofallnow.org) and this book, you will have more than enough information to make decisions and act on them.

# SECTION A: *Who am I? Who are We?*

## 1. MYTH—STORIES OF HUMANKIND

In *The Power of Myth*, a book, and hugely popular series of televised conversations on American television in 1988, the author Joseph Campbell gave the American audience a real appreciation for the Power of Myth and the Hero's Journey. These stories are the touchstones of human culture and existence told since the time we first learned to communicate verbally.

Homer's epic poem the Odyssey may indeed be familiar to many— Wikipedia notes that experts around the world declared the Odyssey "literature's most enduring narrative" (https://en.wikipedia.org/wiki/ Odyssey). Current examples like *The Wizard of Oz, Star Wars, The Lord of the Rings,* and the Harry Potter stories, are also myths. Myths describe how any one of us, if our heart is in the right place, can achieve extraordinary outcomes. The hero's power grows from the pursuit of a worthy goal, a better world, and the companionship of a team of trusted fellow travelers. The lesson of the journey unlocks the power of the myth, which often turns out to be already inside us.

Like Odysseus, Frodo, Luke Skywalker, and Dorothy, you will uncover how to develop your superpowers. In *The Wizard of Oz*, as many readers will recall, Dorothy, her dog Toto, and their three companions all have a purpose: Dorothy needs to get home, the Tin Man needs a heart, the Scarecrow needs a brain, the Lion needs courage, and Toto pulls back the curtain to reveal the Wizard so that they may all return home triumphant. Chapter 1 is about the path and finding the *heart* to embark on the quest. Chapter 2 is about gaining the *wisdom* to make the choices, even if they are difficult. Chapter 3 is about having the *courage* to act on the compassionate loving voice of the heart and the insight that comes from wisdom and, Chapter 4 reveals the triumphant outcome: "... at the end of the road is a golden sky And the sweet silver song of a lark." (Gerry Marsden MBE 1942-2021, "You'll Never Walk Alone"). Consider this your personal invitation. What a trip! RSVP requested. www. forthegoodofallnow.org

## 2. POWER-*OVER*—POWER-*WITH*

These four words will shift your understanding of the world and the place of humanity in it, and they will guide us through the coming macroshift to the paradigm of *holos*—oneness. In time, you will be able to immediately determine whether a particular undertaking is going to result in the Good of All, or the Good of the Few. Every day you make decisions to use power-*over* or power-*with*. Become aware of your thoughts and actions as they relate to these two kinds of power. As you observe, you will notice that power-*over* leads toward separation and domination, whereas power-*with* leads toward Unity and Peace— harmony. Power-*over* drains your energy. Power-*with* creates synergy— meaning it creates an energy that is greater than the sum of its parts— the energy in harmony, unity and peace.

No amount of power-*over* is going to save those who wield it because no man-made power-*over* can compete for long against nature's power-*with*. The passage through the *macroshift* will be achieved by moving away from power-*over* and toward power-*with*. It is difficult to understand how any person would willingly want to be responsible for massive anthropogenic (human caused) disruption to life on Earth. Yet this is the deadly course our current 'leaders' are on. If the 'leaders' are taking us over a cliff, must we follow? Of course not. While billions of people all over the world take to the streets and corridors of power every day to try to influence policy and to prevent or lessen this catastrophe, often risking their lives to do so, there are many, many more on the sidelines, at least for now. There are also those who see the *"world ...as... a commodity... whose...heart...was small, and hard, and full of meanness."* They will use all the power-*over* they can arouse to defeat power-*with*, and although their strategies may no longer work, beware of the thrashing tail of the dying dinosaur as it seeks to retain power-*over*.

## 3. SHARED FATES, SHARED SPIRIT and RIGHT RELATIONSHIP

In the era of the Cult of Individualism, which I will cover in more detail later, it is a challenge for many to recognize that we are completely interconnected, but we are. You will find the following three themes— shared fates, spirit, and right relationship to each other and nature— echoing throughout For the Good of All, NOW! I believe, as the Indigenous cultures maintain, that these three connections apply to all that exists on Earth and in our universe.

**Shared Fates:** On a basic level, it is clear that we share a common fate: we are born into physical life, and we die. When Joni Mitchell sang "We Are Stardust" at Woodstock in 1969, she was not just artistically correct, she was also scientifically correct. Everything in our physical world is made from stardust and it returns to stardust—from dust to dust. We know that our universe was created from a single point in a Big Bang occurring about 13.8 billion years ago. The big bang of light and energy expanded to form the universe we live in. As it stretched out, it cooled down. As the universe cooled, it yielded the basic building blocks of all matter—the atom and its sub-particles.

In an interview by Simon Worrall, published January 28, 2015 in *National Geographic*, the authors Karel and Iris Schrijver of *Living with the Stars—How the Human Body is Connected to the Life Cycles of the Earth, the Planets, and the Stars*, state that "Everything we are and everything in the universe and on Earth originated from stardust, ...and it finds its way into plants, and from there into the nutrients that we need for everything we do—think, move, grow." **(**See link at www.forthegoodofallnow.org**)** A human being is inseparable from the molecules, the stardust, we are all made of. We cannot escape that we are made of the same physical materials that we share with the universe and with 8 billion people on Earth.

Our shared *fate* is quite different from our shared *fates,* the tangible sense that our lives and wellbeing depend on other creatures like our families, groups, and communities. For most of the time pre-humans and humans have existed on earth, shared fates have provided the basis for the formation of norms and behaviors that we refer to as culture and values. In the modern world, this sense is revived in times of great danger when people willingly give aid and sustenance to each other and even strangers, because of a sense that we're all in the same boat.

**Spirit:** There are countless reasons to believe in spirit despite the popular modern rejection of its existence because some claim no one can prove that it exists. Yet, we generally accept that consciousness exists, even if no one can describe the physical properties of consciousness, because there are no physical properties. We did not understand electricity though it existed before we were able to discern how and why it works. Just because no one can actually define what, where, and how spirit and consciousness exist, doesn't mean there is no such thing as spirit and consciousness.

Like many people, I believe spirit is something like an energy wave. It is the light of the Big Bang; where it came from is unknown, but it has always been. The Big Bang gave birth to all the stars, the earth, planets, and molecules in our universe. Our instinctive, universal veneration of light—sun, moon, stars, lightning and fire—is all connected to energy. Our ancient human ancestors intuitively connected to light as the source of spirits and gods. Many of these myths can be found in the rites, celebrations, and customs that predate the birth of the major religions and cultures. The rejection of the notion that we are at once spiritual and physical beings is a *very* recent phenomenon in terms of humanity's history. Despite the preponderance of evidence that spirit is an essential part of human nature observed in every ancient culture, some remain stubbornly opposed to one of the foundational truths of what it means to be human and natural. They claim that unless there is scientific proof, spirit does not exist. This is like saying atoms didn't exist until science proved it, or the earth was flat until it was proven to be round. The purpose of science is to unravel these mysteries. Today we know the world is round and that atoms exist. So, let's put the deceptive claim that spirit doesn't exist to bed with the help of two of the world's most accomplished Nobel Prize winning scientists:

"Consciousness cannot be accounted for in physical terms. For consciousness is absolutely fundamental. It cannot be accounted for in terms of anything else."

—Erwin Schrödinger

"Everyone who is seriously engaged in the pursuit of science becomes convinced that the laws of nature manifest the existence of a spirit vastly superior to that of men, and one in the face of which we with our modest powers must feel humble."

—Albert Einstein

Our thoughts, dreams, visions, and intuitions are interwoven with our human consciousness which in turn exists in a broader field of consciousness commonly called the cosmos, the spiritual world. This will be the truth for the future human, just as plain as the world is round.

**Right Relationship:** Humans live in a state of interrelationship with each other and the entire natural system we live in. This should be evident in this time of climate chaos. When the land dries up, the water becomes scarce, the air makes us sick, pandemics kill hundreds of millions of people, wildfires rage, seas rise, weather becomes increasingly dangerous, and species die off at an alarming rate, all as a result of the destruction of nature by humans, we cannot claim that our relationship to life on this planet has been, in recent history, hospitable or caring. Yet, there is nothing in our life that is not interdependent, interconnected, interrelated with the world we live in. Those who seek to deny this are simply lying to you in order to gain some benefit for themselves. They are exploiting you. This exploitation is constant and culturally sanctioned, and it is bringing us close to extinction. Billions of people are rebelling and resisting these practices.

Ultimately, every person on earth is going to experience, physically and spiritually, what it means to have artificially separated our wellbeing from the wellbeing of the planet, and from the environment that sustains all life on Earth. I am writing this book to demonstrate why we should not be running away from this paradigm shift, but greeting it with open arms as the opportunity for a glorious new future. There is a choice, but it is a false choice, because the flip side of this vision is not really an option at all. The path ahead is clear what becomes of us is largely based on our actions for better or worse.

The Quaker faith-community in the United States has thought deeply about the issue of Right Relationship, which they use to describe what they aspire to achieve while living on earth. Peter G. Brown and Geoffrey Garver, in a paper called "Humans and Nature: The Right Relationship" provide a compelling definition of right relationship: "A thing is right when it tends to preserve the integrity, resilience, and beauty of the commonwealth of life. It is wrong when it tends otherwise." (See link at www.forthegoodofallnow.org) We have drifted a long way from this definition, and the impacts are about to be felt.

*Humanity's relationship as the prime exploiter of nature will either change or result in extinction.*

## 4. YIN AND YANG

The Eastern traditions have long understood the sense of the duality and balance found in the universe and nature. The common taijitu symbol—a circle, divided equally in tear drop shaped halves, one black—the Yin; one white—the Yang, with a black dot in the white half and white dot in the black half. Symbolically it represents the relationship of duality or opposites in nature: day (Yang)—night (Yin). Yin is the dark, feminine, moon, water, cold, passive, enlightenment. Yang is the white, masculine, sky, hot, aggressive. And yet, it symbolizes that everything co-exists in the circle of life. Yin and Yang are at once created by and created from its own energy—qi. The part is the whole and the whole is the part. This is somewhat counter-intuitive, because in school we learn that the whole is the sum of the parts. But nature is made of parts that are organized in holarchies, in levels (hierarchy) of parts (called holons) that make the whole (holarchy). My lung is an organ that is made of tissues, cells and molecules but it can't exist without the molecules that exist in the cells, and the cells that exist in the tissues, and in the tissues that make up my lung. (See Resources at www.forthegoodofallnow.org.) It is critically important because it highlights the interconnectedness of everything in nature. The stardust in me is the same as the stardust in you and the stardust in a rock, a tree, or a dog. And we are all animated by the same energy. The idea that we are separate from each other, and nature is incorrect. And this compels a re-evaluation of interconnection of humans Right Relationship to each other and nature.

The scientists are at least a hundred years ahead of the mainstream population. The idea that nature is arranged in geometric or mathematical building blocks came from the Ancient Greeks. Their amazing advances in the sciences provided the foundations for scientific inquiry ever since! It provided the Einsteins and Schrödingers the ability to eventually determine that instead of building blocks, nature looks more like sheets of different colors undulating in waves across the universe. The paper you are touching is made up of atoms arrayed in those waves. An atom vibrating at one end of the universe is capable of making a quantum leap, causing atoms to vibrate at the other end of the universe.

There are some very powerful forces at work in this epic time of transition named the *Great Turning*, by Joanna Macy. Climate adaptation will be necessary if the human race is to survive. Humans all over the world are sensing and reacting to this momentous change because we are interconnected in a vast web as physical and spiritual beings governed by the laws of nature and manifesting "the existence of a spirit vastly superior to that of men." (*Coming Back to Life,* Macy J. and Young Brown, M.) Current global trends toward authoritarianism will continue to rise. It is not necessary or smart to fall for such a negative response when there are positive alternatives. We've been accustomed for centuries to entrust our welfare to our so-called 'leaders,' be they tyrants or goodhearted people. There are tremendous forces and energy at work co-creating a future world order where *We the People* will use new simple tools for the self-management of our communities, as described in this manual. Our personal engagement with life will determine a future where the wellbeing of all is the ultimate measure of a life well lived.

# SECTION B: *Where am I Going?*

## 1. EVOLUTION & ADAPTATION

Humans, like all species, are constantly evolving and adapting. This process of evolution makes us who we are, what we are, and why we do many of the things we do. It is also what makes a fish a fish, an oak an oak, and a butterfly a butterfly. Nature is constantly evolving, and we are part of nature. We have no choice in this matter from a genetic and biological viewpoint. What we often refer to as instincts are patterns of behavior cultivated by our responses to the incentives, catalysts, motivations developed and refined by evolution. Perhaps the most commonly known of these genetic 'instincts' are the reactions we share with many animals when in danger: Fight, Flight, Freeze and the less commonly mentioned, Feign.

Long before we emerged as Homo *sapiens*, going back a million years or so, our predecessors formed groups containing multiple generations who lived together and cared for each other. Much like the great apes and bonobos do to this day. They also exhibited, like ants and apes, clear divisions of labor and dominance hierarchies—think of a queen bee, for example. While many other species shared these traits of multi-generational "nesting"—kinship, work assignments, specific duties, responsibilities, and caring for each other—only one species mastered fire and only one species mastered three key attributes, as described by E.O. Wilson in *The Social Conquest of Earth*: shared attention; the awareness that a common goal could be achieved through cooperation; and a "theory of mind" that their mental states could be shared by others in the group. Sometime prior to 60,000 years ago, humans developed language, forever differentiating the new Homo species from all other animals. Fire changed our physical being. Awareness changed our relationship to each other and the world we lived in. Sometime between 15,000 to 40,000 years ago only one species of the many pre-human branches we descended from would survive: Homo *sapiens—sapiens* means *wise*.

Adaptation is an essential and complex part of the way nature acts at multiple levels—individual and group, genes and cultures. One of the main purposes of adaptation is to ensure that the species will successfully survive, reproduce and grow. Successful adaptations require abandoning processes that damage the survival chances of the group while selecting genetic and/or cultural processes to ensure the species will survive and multiply. The awareness that species are continuously adapting to ensure the continuity of the system, even if it means self-regulating the size of the herd, is one example of the extreme sophistication of a system far more complex than anything humans could have designed, built or reproduced. And even as we are awed by this ability to adapt, we also know that entire species have gone and are going extinct at an alarming pace today because they failed to adapt to a changing environment. Evolution is not always pretty. Humans are not so exceptional as to be exempt from the consequences of failing to adapt. The human existential crisis we hear so much about today,—meaning our very existence as a species is at risk—is <u>not</u> just drama.

The social scientist and author of *Promise Ahead* and *Voluntary Simplicity*, Duane Elgin, would ask audiences, "How grown up do you think humanity is? ... A toddler? A teenager? A young adult? An elder?" Did you answer 'teenager'? This was the most common answer and presents a useful analogy. Humanity is going through its rite of passage from adolescence to adulthood—this is the period where growth is the biological imperative; a time of plenty of excitement and chaos! Although the impending changes will affect *everyone*, some will resist change with all their might. The adolescent humanity, like the adolescent human, is figuring out and testing the limits of their power and prowess. They are learning from experience.

The increasing chaos that comes from human activities is part of an evolutionary 'radar' system warning. If our species is to survive climate change and possibly nuclear self-destruction, we will have to evolve in a way that chooses to protect and repair the natural systems we depend on for life. In other words, we had better develop a right relationship with the ecosystem that sustains our species. Nature is not going to end, even if *we* seem intent on racing toward extinction. Despite the noble efforts of billions of people protesting, resisting and lobbying, the people and institutions that hold power-*over* are unable to rebalance the current system that seeks endless growth and is designed for the benefit *Of the Few* rather than the wellbeing *Of All*.

**An ideology that preserves good For the Good of the Few, will not survive the adaptation to the new ideology of For the Good of All.**

This book pays witness to the belief that our species has both the wisdom and compassion to act For the Good of All, NOW! and that what is needed is a new strategy and a broad, local-to-global coalition of people empowered individually and communally to make change happen from the bottom up. We will adapt like we have throughout our long history as a species. The survival of Homo *sapiens* is not limited to any particular ethnicity, race, color, nationality, wealth, education, or any other differentiating factor. The pull of species self-preservation will get stronger as the chaos in nature and human society increases. What turn our future takes depends on our combined action or our combined failure to take action. However, don't assume the 'leaders' will lead, nor that nature will recalibrate magically. Like teenagers who believe themselves to be invincible, these 'leaders' disregard danger warnings and push the limits. They are constantly moving the goalposts while assuring us that we just need a little more time to get this under control. They won't. The constellation of crises—the melting poles, glaciers, and the permafrost, drought, disasters, famine, pandemics, fierce storms, rising oceans, fires, war—are likely to get worse before they get better. As Einstein famously told us: "Insanity is doing the same thing over and over again and expecting different results."

As called for in *For the Good of All NOW!* and in many other quarters, it is time to tie all these bright strands together to gain the synergy of concerted and effective action everywhere, but especially in communities where we can make change happen NOW!

## 2. MACROSHIFT

In *Macroshift: Navigating the Transformation to a Sustainable World,* Professor Ervin Laszlo describes a *macroshift* as a sweeping global-level paradigm shift. A macroshift, goes beyond a typical paradigm shift, both refer to a significant transformation of culture, society, beliefs, values, behaviors, customs and norms. But a macroshift is more than that, it is global in nature and results in a major evolutionary transition. Even lesser changes are wrenching and often violent, and societies experience the stress. In a macroshift, the whole world seems topsy-turvy. Understanding that this is not the first macroshift, but the fourth signals that humans are strong and flexible—resilient. That resilience is part of the human history of a million years of adaptation. We can do this.

**Mythos:** In the time of *mythos,* our pre-human ancestors were part of a mythical natural world filled with spirits and magical forces. A subtle separation starts to occur at the end of this period as evidenced in cave paintings, monuments, and artifacts all pointing to a culture that was increasingly sophisticated and deeply intertwined, in a state of awe and oneness with the natural world. The center of group living was around the circle of campfire, and this is where the budding human would socialize. There is evidence that our pre-human predecessors established bonds of kinship and caring—that there was *compassion* in their social groups. By the end of this era, the species known as Homo *sapiens* had migrated in several waves out of Africa to become the dominant human species on earth.

**Theos:** The second macroshift, *theos,* arose roughly 10,000 years ago when humans began to settle in societies—small camps and villages and eventually cities and civilizations. These larger and more complex societies evolved into religious-states—*theocracies*. They were organized "as above, so below", in hierarchies. Just as humans perceived the gods above them, they perceived themselves to be above all the other creatures around them which was also organized in *hierarchy* by rank and class. Homo *sapiens* was definitely above and unlike the other living species and nature around them, physically and spiritually. The oneness of humans with all living things during *mythos* was gradually replaced in favor of the belief that a special human status existed above and apart from the rest of the natural world, especially in the Western World.

**Logos:** The third macroshift—*logos*—unfolds in two distinct parts. I leave out the rich history of the East to focus on the West because *logos* became a hallmark of the Eurocentric ethic that started to dominate world affairs by the mid-19th century. The early *logos* period emerged around 1200 BCE built on the flourishing Phoenician, Greek, and Roman empires. By the late *logos* period, instead of beliefs alone defining our world, our reason (logic) and science defines it. Humans start to live by rules and measurable standards governing morality and society. *Eurocentrism:* The ancient civilizations of Greece (science and philosophy), Phoenicia (seafaring, trade), and Rome (the basis for the modern state) set the foundation for the rise of Eurocentrism—a worldview that reflects European history, economics, government, culture, and values. By the 1400s, a new wave of advances built on the legacies of these earlier cultures rapidly replaced long held convictions like the "earth is flat," while introducing an outburst of advances in navigation, mathematics, physics, mechanics, engineering, art, law, justice, and professional governance.

Language and customs begin to reflect what we call a national identity today. By the 1600s, Europeans were colonizing vast territories in the East and West. *Colonialism* was extremely profitable for the Europeans but disastrous for local native populations—Indigenous peoples—who were killed by war, disease, persecution, and forced migrations (displacement), including the mass enslavement and deportation of Africans, while their natural resources were plundered.

**Holos:** By the mid-to-late 1700s, Eurocentrism would replace the divine right of kings and the feudal system, to give rise to nationalism, democracy, and capitalism. The religion of Eurocentrism was Christianity, though its influence on secular life would eventually fade in many Western countries. Capitalism was deemed to have started with the publication in 1776, of Adam Smith's *An Inquiry into the Nature and Causes of the Wealth of Nations,* in which he asserted that "The great object of the Political Economy of every country is to increase the riches and power of that country." The territorial conquests of colonialism supplied the raw materials to fuel nationalism, industrialization, and capitalism. By the 20th century, growth had become the prime directive for economies and Adam Smith's invisible 'iron fist'—essentially the guardrails of morality to contain man's worst excesses—had given way to the embrace of 'free markets.' The responsibility of businesses was and is to maximize revenues for the benefit of the owners or shareholders. The responsibility of governments was and is to support the wealth of nations and the companies that created it. The responsibility of individuals evolved into the pursuit of 'happiness' in the context of rank and status in the hierarchy. Ultimately, and especially in the U.S., from the mid-1960s onward the rising irrational beliefs in the superiority of markets, that good government meant small government, and that the individual had an almost unlimited right to seek happiness took root though it remained a highly subjective right as it operated on the basis of rank, sex, status and skin color.

Consistent with Adam Smith's framework, growth would become the highest priority of human activity. The pursuit of supposedly unending growth immediately started choking the life out of the planet. In 1856, Eunice Foote who studied the heat effect of carbon dioxide trapped under glass, determined that pollution could result in a warming of the planet. Denying the climate impact of pollution goes back a long way! Today's greenhouse effect on global temperatures and weather has been compared, because of the potential impact, to the five previous mass extinctions going back 440 million years. The last one, about 65 million years ago, was caused by a heat trapping cloud that encircled the globe and may have been caused by an asteroid or meteor storm. One hundred and thirty years after Eunice Foote's discovery, in June 1988, NASA Director James Hansen warned the world about the greenhouse effect. Thirty-four years later, the growth economies of the world continue to pollute our atmosphere and our 'leaders' continue to demonstrate their impotence to do much about it. The recent United Nations 26th Council of Parties (COP26) in 2021, which was billed as a planetary red-alarm moment, laid bare how unlikely it will be for the world's 'leaders' to effectively achieve much to delay or reduce the impacts of the potential Sixth Mass Extinction as a result of a heat trapping cloud produced by human industrial and capitalist activity.

In *Collapse: How Societies Choose to Fail or Succeed* (2005), Jared Diamond suggests that throughout history five factors have contributed to social collapse: (i) climate change, (ii) hostile neighbors, (iii) collapse of essential trading partners, (iv) environmental problems, and (v) society's response to these four factors. In particular, Jared Diamond identifies the two main causes for past civilization collapse, which are, the failure to engage in long-term planning and the unwillingness to reconsider core values. The good news is that we can also implement world systems for the good of the planet and all its people.

*Every macroshift involves a transformation of humanity's
relationship to each other and to Nature.*

Laszlo describes the 4th *Macroshift* as moving "from national industrial societies toward a globally interdependent yet locally diverse world." Joanna Macy named it **The Great Turning** a paradigm shift "from the Industrial Growth Society to a Life-sustaining Society." *(Coming Back to Life—Practice to Reconnect Our Lives, Our World,* Joanna Macy and Molly Young Brown, 1998) See links to this work at www.forthegoodofallnow.org)

## 3. THE BUTTERFLY EFFECT

The Industrial Revolutions, the first in the 1750s—steam, iron, textiles in Great Britain, the second, from the 1850s onward—steel, electricity, automobiles, and the oil-economy in the U.S., led to the self-inflicted and disastrous effects of climate change. Our world is a highly complex system. When complex systems get out of balance, even the tiniest fluctuations can have outsized impacts. This is the finding of a weather scientist named Lorenz who famously described this as *the butterfly effect*—a flap of the butterfly's wings in the Amazon causes a thunderstorm in Siberia.

*Tiny fluctuations in complex systems can have outsized impacts.*

Pumping our atmosphere full of particles and gasses—the ones that are in coal, oil and gas formed over millennia by decomposing vegetative matter into carbon—may not result in devastation equal to the impact of any of the five previous mass extinctions on earth, but what we are experiencing now, in terms of the impacts of climate change, are just the early stages of climate chaos. The thawing of the permafrost—the land mass around the North Pole—will release enough trapped methane gas to *double the amount of carbon dioxide* in the atmosphere! This will be disastrous and will set the stage for a mass extinction. And while this has been known for quite some time, our 'leaders' have proven that they are incapable of making the hard choices to change course. To this day, the world still subsidizes Big Oil! But that doesn't leave us helpless, *We the People*, have an enormous capacity to adapt.

> *"Never doubt that a small group of thoughtful,*
> *committed citizens can change the world; indeed,*
> *it's the only thing that ever has."*

—Margaret Mead

Our refuge will be in the shelter of each other, in community. Although there will be long-term damage and it will take time to recover from the impacts of human-induced climate change, there are self-correcting mechanisms that will do what the 'leaders' are not capable of doing— putting the brakes on industrial growth, big agriculture, and consumerism that are adding fuel to the fire. I am speaking of the impacts of war, economic collapse, and climate disasters that will dramatically slow the polluting activities that are already wreaking havoc around the world.

Nature itself is rebelling at the uncaring and harmful behaviors of Homo *sapiens*. The ecological systems are adapting to climate change (see the 2016 IUCN Climate Change report). Species survive as a result of successful genetic self-preservation responses. Are we adapting? In a period of fluctuating climate conditions, Greenland experienced a 10°C (50°F) rise in temperature in ten years! OK, so that was between 20,000 and 40,000 years ago. (See www.forthegoodofallnow.org for a link to an interactive tool showing the rise of temperatures globally since 1884. It is eye-opening.) No one is talking about a global 10°C degree rise, but often all we seem focused on is a rising thermometer. Let's focus more on the *impacts* on our communities. Because it is not just about temperature, it is about being prepared for more frequent and damaging disasters, it is about our response to the mass migrations of people escaping the huge, no longer livable, spaces on either side of the equator and other areas no longer able to sustain the human herd with the food and water necessary for life. We cannot take a pill and make the threat to our species go away. The signals that something radically wrong is happening beyond the terms of the cyclical social and cultural commotion can be made real by playing with the interactive tool mentioned above and by paying attention to the currents of unrest, not just the latest breaking news.

If the prevailing systems of government are incapable of preserving the species, then our survival is based on replacing those systems. Nature is already dealing with the chaos of systemic imbalances. Human cultural responses are playing catch-up. It is tempting to throw up our hands and give up to these forces that are so much bigger than we are. But, even in that despair, the seeds of hope are sprouting and each of us can acquire the superpowers we need. It is time for a bold new strategy and a rapid expansion of participation to make change happen faster. I will describe in the following pages how *We the People* can bypass the steadfast waffling and wavering of the 'leaders' and take matters into our own hands NOW!

## 4. THE FOURTH TURNING

*The Fourth Turning* is the title of a compelling history of the cyclical nature of time and human activity by William Strauss and Neil Howe, and it brings into focus what is happening now, how we should prepare for major change, and when the end of the current era will occur. (Resources: www.forthegoodofallnow.org)

The prevailing notion of time in Western culture is that it is linear. However, most cultures understand that the wheels of time turn, break, reconnect and turn again. The focus of the Fourth Turning traces these cycles back 3000 years. Each Turning of the wheel lasts what the Romans referred to as a 'saeculum' (pronounced seck-u-lum)—roughly a long life of 80 to 100 years. This eventually became the standard century, by which Europeans and now most of the world marks history. Laszlo's *logos* civilization starts in the 1400s corresponding roughly to Strauss and Howe's Anglo-American Era. I will be referring to this period as the Eurocentric era or Western culture.

| The Anglo-American Era | | Crisis Year | (length of saeculum) |
|---|---|---|---|
| Late Medieval | 1435-1487 | 1485 War of the Roses | (52 years) |
| Reformation | 1487-1594 | 1588 Armada Crisis | (107 years) |
| New World | 1594-1704 | 1689 Glorious Revolution | (110 years) |
| Revolutionary War | 1704-1794 | 1781 American Revolution | (90 years) |
| Civil War | 1794-1865 | 1863 Civil War | (71 years) |
| Great Power | 1865-1946 | 1944 Great Depression/ WWII | (81 years) |
| Millennial | 1946 -2026? | 1946 *Pax Americana* | (80 years) |

## The Four Turnings of Millennial Period 1946-2026

Typically, each Turning has four segments. It starts on a *High*, moves to an *Awakening* then to an *Unraveling* and, finally it ends in a *Crisis*. Then it starts again. I will refer to the current cycle, called the Millennial period by Strauss and Howe, which they called the Millennial and I call the *Pax Americana*—American Peace.

i.  **First Turning:** *the* *High*-**1946-1964** (18 years)—is called *The American High:* the upbeat post war era is typified by Kennedy's willingness to put a man on the moon! [Compares to *Gilded Age* 1865-1886]

ii. **Second Turning:** *the* *Awakening*-**1964-1984** (20 Years) *The Consciousness Revolution:* new values seek to replace the old ones; 60s and 70s counterculture of raised 'consciousness', assassinations of JFK, RFK and MLK; 1969 Apollo 11 landing on the moon! [Compares to *Great Awakening* 1886-1908]

iii. **_Third Turning:_** *the Unraveling*—**1984-2009\*** (25 years) *The Culture Wars:* strengthening individualism, weakening institutionalism—small government; anti-war (Viet Nam), anti-draft, Students for a Democratic Society; race riots; 9/11/2001 bombing of the World Trade Center * 2009 is my chosen end-date. *The Fourth Turning* was published in 1997. [Compares to WWI and Prohibition—1908-1929; 21 years.]

iv. **_Fourth Turning:_** *the Crisis*—**2009-2026** (17 years) _Collapse or Rebirth:_ marked by upheaval and a break with past values and a social order. Public power is at its lowest ebb, except in short breakthroughs. Private corporate and individual power reign for a while longer. [Compares to the Great Depression and WWII -1929-1946; 17 years] The invasion of Ukraine marks the end of the relative peace called *Pax Americana*. It is the turning point for the final stage of the *Crisis* Interestingly, in 1997, Strauss and Howe predicted 2025 as the end of the Millennial Era!

## The *Crisis* Period—2009-2026—Collapse or Rebirth

I repeat for the sake of clarity, that my focus is on the collapse of the Eurocentric *ethos*—the culture, beliefs, customs and spirit of an era. The U.S. is the dominant global representative of this ethic today. The focus of my attention is on what is happening in the U.S., as the leading member Western culture in this saeculum. Like any culture there are regional similarities and differences, but the reverberations of what happens in the U.S. will play out globally making this a macroshift, as opposed to just a civilizational shift.

**Cycle 1: The Catalyst 2009-2020 (11 years)**—*a sudden shift in mood*—Two events in 2008-2009 changed America—the election of the first Black president in American history and the Great Recession. Both breathe life into grievance over the loss of White status and the toxic revived White Replacement theory, a nonsensical fear-driven belief that there is a conspiracy to get rid of White people. The election of Donald Trump in 2016 preys on this grievance, giving rise to a significant White nationalist, racist, and autocratic movement, inflamed by disinformation. The obvious historical comparison to all of this is to the prewar rise of Nazism and the rise of Mussolini and Hitler in 1920s and 30s.

**Cycle 2: The Regeneracy 2020-2022 (2 years)** *re-energized civic life:* The failure of the autocratic Trump to seize control of the U.S. in the January 6, 2021, coup is an extraordinary success for democracy. Many countries would have faltered. By 2022, despite all the challenges, Biden managed to deliver a $1 trillion pandemic rescue plan and a $1 trillion infrastructure plan. Both parties operate in the paradigm of power-*over*, but only Republicans are openly inciting revolution.

**Cycle 3: The Climax 2022-2024 (2 years)** *an obvious break with the past:* "Whatever sparks the change, it will lead to the resistance of the old order using every means possible to retain its status, while the new order seeks change." There are two catalysts that mark an obvious break with the past: the January 6, 2021, failed coup in the U.S. and the end of the post-world war *Pax Americana* (American Peace) that began in 1946 and is unraveling now (February 24, 2022) as Russia invaded Ukraine. Both offer strong examples of obvious breaks, and both mark the decline and fall of Eurocentrism.

Russia is trying to recreate the old order of Empire, the era of the Tsars and Tsarinas that began in the mid-1500s and which, after the Russian Revolution, became known as the Soviet Union (1922). Ukraine was incorporated in the post-war Soviet Union. As Hitler did in the 1930s in Germany, Putin uses grievance as the *means* to achieve his aim of amassing power-*over*. Putin has been promoting for decades Russian grievance about its loss of status as a world power after the breakup of the Soviet Union. Grievance has long been a powerful tool of tyrants and autocrats to arouse the masses. Nationalism and fascism are its modern-day champions. Trump has been using White grievance to stoke nationalism (fascism) and racism on the national stage since at least 2008. We think revolution can't happen in the U.S., but there is a sizable portion of the population that wants nothing less. Just as importantly, the Republican Party has embraced Trump and the notion that the clock can be turned back to the 1950s, or 1850s for that matter. The Italians never thought Mussolini would succeed. The Germans never believed Hitler would succeed. Is the United States simply going to replay the cycle of history? The Union survived the Civil War, but will it survive another breakup (secession)?

The next flash points will come quickly. Some or all of the following events are imaginable: the war in Ukraine will become increasingly destructive and dangerous, and the use of nuclear weapons is conceivable if Putin needs to save face; cyber warfare attacks on Europe and the U.S. are met with retaliation; the cracks in globalization supply chains, food, oil, and other natural resources will lead to worldwide misery; financial systems and national economies will become destabilized, leading to deglobalization; and all the while climate disasters will become more frequent and more destructive. In the U.S., the 2022 midterm elections will be a disaster with both parties disputing the results; the referee in the previous election fiasco—Bush v Gore, 2000—was the U.S. Supreme Court. Just as the appointment of justices has been cheapened, politicized and corrupted, the Court is now the political tool of one party instead of the impartial referee the founders had hoped for. It is an obvious part of a long steady crumbling of social, economic, judicial, political, and institutional effectiveness that will be too weak and unadaptable to survive. This has created the perfect storm for a disputed election to turn into secession or outright revolution. States will start the process to secede (break away) from the Union. This will cause tidal wave shifts in geo-political and global economic terms. Most notably, it will either launch or be a significant part of a global financial system collapse occurring sometime around 2022-2023, which Strauss and Howe referred to as the *Great Devaluation.* Because global economies are so intertwined, the effect will be far more serious than the Great Depression (1929). Any one of these possibilities will be enough to set the U.S. and the world on a new trajectory.

**Cycle 4: The Resolution 2024-2026 (2 years)**—*a new trajectory:* In 1997, Strauss and Howe predicted that the resolution of the *Crisis* would end in 2025. Although many people will focus on this date, I urge you to remember that it really doesn't matter. The only reason for attempting to predict future events is to allow time to prepare. The pretense of the 'leaders' and elites that, once the Covid-19 pandemic is over, all will return to normal, to more growth, to more globalization, is at best brash optimism or more likely self-deceit, or bold propaganda. In times of chaos, the unpredictable will happen. War, economic failures leading to recession and inflation, the fragmenting of a *dis*-United States, and deglobalization, occurring in the midst of climate related disasters bringing death, famine and increasing forced migration, will all play roles. As the U.S. goes through the *Resolution* period, these deep fissures will reverberate through the global economic, political and social systems like a *tsunami*, creating the tidal wave of the *Holos* macroshift. Whether it ends in a *Collapse,* an *In-Between* period, or a *Breakthrough,* one thing is certain: the passage through to the next chapter in the history of humankind, the transition to holos, *will depend on the empowered engagement of people working together, not institutions.*

# SECTION C: *How am I and How are We Getting There?*

### "The Guest Inside You"
### By Kabir

The Guest is inside you, and also inside me;
you know the sprout is hidden inside the seed.
We are all struggling; none of us has gone far.
Let your arrogance go, and look around inside.
The blue sky opens out farther and farther,
the daily sense of failure goes away,
the damage I have done to myself fades,
a million suns come forward with light,
when I sit firmly in that world.
I hear bells ringing that no one has shaken,
inside "love" there is more joy than we know of,
rain pours down, although the sky is clear of clouds,
there are whole rivers of light.
The universe is shot through in all parts by a single sort of love.
How hard it is to feel that joy in all our four bodies!
Those who hope to be reasonable about it fail.
The arrogance of reason has separated us from that love.
With the word "reason" you already feel miles away.
How lucky Kabir is, that surrounded by all this joy
he sings inside his own little boat.
His poems amount to one soul meeting another.
These songs are about forgetting dying and loss.
They rise above both coming in and going out."

From: *Kabir—Ecstatic Poems* by Robert Bly

*There is potentiality inside everything and everyone*
*if we are humble enough to invite in.*

Six hundred years ago Kabir wrote about potentiality: "You know the sprout is hidden inside the seed." He describes far better than I do, what happens as a result: his "daily sense of failure' and his self-inflicted "damage" fade away; a "million suns" shine, "bells" ring; he finds a "universe...of love"; and "The blue sky opens out farther and farther and we let our 'arrogance go." We are able to "look around inside." We choose to seek and find our own wisdom.

# 1. THE FIVE POWERS—*TRUE POWER*

### *Love and Compassion open the door to all five Powers*

Each chapter will reveal one or more of the five powers from *The Art of Power*, Thich Nhat Hanh (see Resources at www.forthegoodofallnow. org). These powers will lead you toward what he called True Power, "the kind of power that brings happiness and not suffering." True Power will not satisfy cravings such as "wealth, fame, sex, fancy food, and lots of sleep." This is a well-worn path that has guided the wise for thousands of years. In the West, however, it will most certainly appear as a "road less traveled by" ("The Road Less Traveled," Robert Frost). Perhaps the biggest obstacle to overcome for a Westerner is the belief that you think you can master the art of power on your own. You can't and you will be perpetuating the very myths that have brought us to the fourth macroshift: the cult of individualism and its warped vision of humanity as the supreme master of nature. Like a mirage in the desert, the cult of individualism is seducing. It turns you away from the culture of power-*with* by nurturing a culture of power-*over*; toward separation and away from interconnection; toward hierarchy (a ranking system), and away from holarchy (made up of holons—a holon is both a part and the whole, Arthur *Koestler The Ghost in the Machine*).

There is no magical solution. The current 'leaders' of our countries and businesses will, for the most part, be of little or no use. The path requires no special skills to get started. It is within reach of just about everyone. For most, it will require a sliver of your time. In return you will find and attract more happiness, more serenity, more self-empowerment and more insight, than you might have ever expected— *even* in the midst of the chaos of the Great Turning. One of the great challenges of the modern era is that we, as a society, have become spectators and delegators. I mean by this that we have outsourced the management of our affairs and the formation of our values mostly to professional politicians and institutional executives. It will be plain to see, if it is not already, why this is not working for most of us or the rest of the planet. You will also learn how truly simple it is to make the few changes necessary to adapt, survive and to thrive in the *holos* paradigm.

## 2. AWARENESS & SELF-BELIEF

The distractions that keep you from developing awareness are unavoidable in a world obsessed with growth. It takes a simple effort of consciousness and a simple practice to develop the skills to be more fully *aware*. The first step is to have self-belief. Have faith in yourself. I am not referring to faith in the traditional Western religious sense, which is primarily an institutional practice designed to maintain power-*over* the members of that religion. Nor the kind of faith that is aroused by grievance and anger—as Gandhi remarked "An eye for an eye leaves the whole world blind." Self-belief is trusting in your power to grow, to bloom, to become your better self, to fulfill your potential. As Kabir wrote, the source of self-belief is already in you: "Let your arrogance go, and look around inside. The blue sky opens out farther and farther, the daily sense of failure goes away."

Although awareness is not technically one of the five powers, cultivating awareness focuses your attention and in this sense, it leads to mindfulness, which is another power. For example, when you become aware that the constant bombardment of messages that use comparison and competition to claim that more 'stuff' will make you happy is in fact making you less happy, your awareness grants you greater perception, which gives you options. (*The Economics of Happiness,* Samdhong Rinpoche in a film by Helena Norberg-Hodge, Steven Gorelick & John Page—see Resources: www.forthegoodofallnow.org). You understand that making you crave *stuff* you don't have or can ill afford leads to frustration and unhappiness. This awareness changes your relationship to buying *stuff*. The capitalists don't want you to be mindful. They prefer you be impulsive—mindless—so that you buy more stuff. They use comparison and competition to make you want more stuff. As the awareness arises in you that real and lasting happiness will not be found in more stuff, the sellers of stuff lose their hold on you. The more awareness you develop the more in-control and more serene you become. The more you focus your awareness on feelings of love and compassion, the more they appear in your life. Love and compassion attract more love and compassion. You become a co-creator of unity and peace. There is no doubt that physical things can make you more comfortable, but physical comfort is not happiness. Happiness is a state of awareness, an experience in your mind, heart and spirit. You experience happiness and serenity internally, spiritually. You experience pleasure and stimulation externally, physically. Both experiences affect you biologically. Being aware empowers you to know the difference. It is relatively easy to acquire the practice of being more aware.

In the story of Our Lady of Unity and Peace, you may have observed that it took one person to mobilize the efforts of many people to radically change the community of Ammiq and its vicinity. It will not be lost on you that generosity and compassion are what drive this story and that the actions of one person can influence the actions of many. Empowerment comes from compassion. Compassion is the portal through which we understand what it literally means: *to suffer together*. Hold the image of Mikhael and Adla Rouhana sipping sugary hot water from a bowl so that strangers could eat. Stop running away from suffering. That's precisely the wrong goal.

*Awareness of our suffering and the suffering of others is what opens us up to joy. True happiness requires true compassion. Compassion is the key to happiness.*

Not worldly goods. Not good looks. Not influence. Not fame. Not popularity. Not stuff. All of this prevents you from being truly aware of your own suffering and the suffering of others. Whatever that suffering is—it is a part of everyone's life. There is a lesson in this wisdom. It may not appear immediately, but keep listening and questioning. The answer will arise. You will no longer seek to avoid suffering because it opens the world up to you. Then you will turn your suffering into an inner strength "the damage I have done to myself fades, a million suns come forward with light, when I sit firmly in that world." I speak from personal experience that the power of self-belief and self-compassion are the critical stepping-stones on the pathway to happiness and serenity. Recognize that this is not something you can do alone.

*"The most intractable problem today is not pollution or technology or war; but the lack of belief that the future is very much in the hands of the individual."*
—Margaret Mead (1901-1978)

Reclaiming a super-empowered sense of self-belief is not achieved alone. The practice of Circle is the ideal pathway to supercharge self-belief.

*When you become aware that you believe in yourself, your future is in your hands.*

# 3. LOVE FORCE—SPIRIT FORCE—*AHIMSA*

*The practice of universal love and compassion is,*
*like Unity and Peace, contagious.*

The French priest, philosopher and paleontologist Teilhard de Chardin (1881-1955) once stated what is common knowledge in the East, but became distorted by our arrogance in the West, he wrote "You are not a human being in search of a spiritual experience. You are a spiritual being immersed in a human experience." De Chardin was considered, like his contemporary Thomas Merton (1915-1968; *The Seven Story Mountain*), to be on the edge of conventional Catholicism, yet the Unitive Theory, as oneness is sometimes called, is alive in Christianity, not heard often enough from the pulpit, but spoken about nonetheless.

In Buddhism, Hinduism, and Jainism the spirit force is called *ahimsa* and it forms the basis for the doctrine of nonviolence. It also undergirds the movement Gandhi launched called *satyagraha*—from *satya*, a word for truth, also implying love and compassion, and *agraha*, a word for firmness, *polite insistence*, which lends a sense of strength—Truth Force or Spirit Force. Dr. Martin Luther King, Jr., who was very much aligned with Gandhi, called it, "love force," stating that "Love is the only force capable of transforming an enemy into a friend." The ethic of nonviolence holds that all things have a spark of divine spiritual energy and, because this is so, when you hurt another, you are hurting yourself. Whether the hurt is expressed in thought or deed, Gandhi considered it violence. Likewise, when you hold peace and compassion in your spirit and heart, you will attract more spirit and love force. This is the path to happiness and serenity.

# SECTION D—*What changes can I expect to experience?*

## 1. TRANSFORMATIVE EXPERIENCE

Professor of philosophy L.A. Paul, in *Transformative Experience*, offers some great advice about coming to terms with transformative experience. As she describes it: All your friends are becoming vampires and they are urging you to become a vampire too. As you debate whether to join them or not, there is no way of knowing if you will feel the same as them as a result of this transformative experience. How do you make up your mind? Dr. Paul suggests the following guidelines:

- Do I want to discover who I will become if I pursue this course of action?

- Can I reasonably expect that my wellbeing will be improved?

- Will I have support and guidance? Or am I on my own?

- If there is anything that suggests that the results would be *"bad for everyone, then it is bad for the decision-maker"*— you. (See Resources www.forthegoodofallnow.org)

On the other hand, if it has a positive effect on others, it will likely have a positive effect on you, and if you are experiencing this transformation in the company of others it becomes something more than the sum of its parts—a positive synergy. When Mahatma Gandhi left his ashram to march three hundred miles to the ocean to harvest salt, a right reserved to the British, the followers who spontaneously joined him were *transformed*. They braved the violence that befell them until they wore down the soldiers trying to stop them from reaching the sea. This act and subsequent interactions would ultimately gain India its independence from Britain. The last Viceroy of India, Lord Mountbatten, wrote of Gandhi's incredible power: "The manifestation of his power as a Mahatma... far transcended mere political authority. It involved the assumption of personal responsibility, which turned the final sacrifice of his life by assassination into a martyrdom." The whole premise of Gandhi's philosophy was based on people taking personal responsibility for themselves and their relationship with others and the world. Though Gandhi is no longer here, he continues to guide us. Though Dr. King Jr. is no longer here, he continues to shine his light on the path. That light and guidance has always contained love, compassion, peace, unity and inspiration and it has always sought to achieve For the Good of All, NOW! Allow yourself the chance of transformative experience that comes as a result of taking personal responsibility, believing in yourself and engaging in a practice of meaningful interrelationship with others.

*Heart Advice:* When Things Fall Apart—Heart Advice for Difficult Times by Buddhist nun, Pema Chödrön (see Resources at www. forthegoodofallnow.org), could have been written as a companion guide for those who are struggling with evolutionary scale change. Rather than fearing and resisting change, lean into it. Just like life happens, this major change is going to happen. The most productive stance is not to flee, freeze or fight, Chödrön instead teaches us to be open to the possibility: "Awakeness is found in our pleasure and our pain, our confusion and our wisdom, available in each moment of our weird, unfathomable, ordinary everyday lives." In this, she is describing a truth about human existence that the Buddha expressed through the Four Noble Truths: Suffering exists. (Suffering is part of what it means to be human.) Suffering arises from "attachment" to desires. (When we resist change, we suffer. "Attachment" is ego.) Suffering ceases when attachment to desire ceases. (Suffering ends when we let go and stop resisting.) Freedom from suffering is possible by practicing the eightfold path. (From birth to death, our actions and ultimate goal are to realize our essential oneness.)

Circle nurtures your inner beauty and health in the shelter of loving companionship. I know of no other vessel that compares to the practice of Circle to nurture and empower the transition to our shared human adulthood. (See Resources www.forthegoodofallnow.org.)

## 2. *NO MAN IS AN ISLAND*

"No man is an island entire of itself; every man is a piece of the continent, a part of the main..." declared the pastor of St. Paul's Cathedral, John Donne, in London in 1642. Yet today, it appears that Eurocentric culture has drifted far from this truth. As if to confirm this, in an article in the *New York Times* entitled "What is the Cause of Social Inequality?" (November 7, 2021), the authors David Graeber and David Wengrow challenge the prevailing belief that hierarchy is the universal arrangement of large social groups as described in their upcoming publication of *The Dawn of Everything*, which will provide convincing examples of large societies exhibiting self-organized social cohesion and functionality, without the need for hierarchies, in ancient (theos era) Mesopotamia, Europe, Mesoamerica, South and North America, offering "proof that a highly egalitarian society has been possible on an urban scale."

## 3. SELF-ACTUALIZATION AND TRANSCENDENCE

In the early 1940s through the early 50s Abraham Maslow developed his now famous Hierarchy of Needs, which is often depicted as a pyramid, starting with basic needs (in two levels: physiological and safety needs), psychological needs (also two levels: belongingness and love, and esteem) and at the top self-fulfillment needs, self-actualization and, in 1971 the addition of transcendence. Maslow recognized that the relationships were much more fluid than the pyramid suggested, and was not fond that this depiction that suggests that in order to achieve higher levels the lower levels have to be met first. In fact, the levels are all quite interactive.

In adding transcendence to the highest level, Maslow referred to it as "...the very highest and most inclusive or holistic levels of human consciousness, behaving and relating, as ends rather than means, to oneself, to significant others, to human beings in general, to other species, to nature, and to the cosmos." A coming together of the physical and spiritual—oneness.

## 4. PURPOSE

In *La Strada*, Frederico Fellini's masterpiece, the Fool tells the simple Gelsomina: "...everything in this world has a purpose. Even this pebble, for example...I don't know what this pebble's purpose is, but it must have one, because if this pebble has no purpose, then everything is pointless. Even the stars!" Finding one's purpose is the great quest we are given in our lifetimes. It is our own mythical Hero's Journey. Purpose defines the core values we live by and imparts meaning and direction to our lives. Finding and abiding by those core values is a constant process. Your purpose may have little to do with *what you do* and everything to do with *why you are here* on Earth. It is not always evident, but if you listen and practice, your purpose or purposes will reveal themselves. Be ready to accept those messages and to act on them, even if you don't know why, even if it is difficult. Your spirit will guide you. Think like an artist rather than engineer, let your imagination soar. Then listen. Because life is indeed pointless if we have no sense of our purpose for being here. There is no greater gift than when your life and your life purposes align. Watch out!

> "...The blue sky opens out farther and farther,
> the daily sense of failure goes away,
> the damage I have done to myself fades,
> a million suns come forward with light,
> when I sit firmly in that world..."
> —Kabir

# SECTION E: BONUS INSPIRATION

**There is no need to reinvent the wheel!** Enjoy *The Eighteen Indigenous Principles* and *The Earth Charter.* Links at www.forthegoodofallnow.org. These are roadmaps for *your* community.

I hope you were inspired by the true story of *Our Lady of Unity and Peace* which shows the capacity of ordinary people to tear down the walls of prejudice, competition, and deep-seated ancient practices in a most unlikely setting—the Middle East.

Most of us believe that tomorrow will be much like today. Nevertheless, most of us also have some idea of history and some idea that it is important to prepare ourselves, our children, our families, our communities and societies, for all sorts of future eventualities, in short to plan ahead. It is not often that we are asked to plan ahead as if our life depended on it. This is when you want to be aware of "The Guest Inside You." You will tap into your self-belief.

I hope Chapter 1 has provided you with some insights, food for thought, and an invitation to join meaningfully in the coming major evolutionary transition. The invitation comes with no strings attached. However, it will involve some sacrifice consisting of 10 to 20 hours of your time over the next 10-12 weeks to gather in the practice of Circle. I suggest that the experience is likely to transform your life and the lives of people around you. There is no catch. You get to keep all that you learn and gain by the experience. Whether you are in the trial period or fully engaged, we do ask participants to consider a small donation (in the U.S., we are suggesting $1 or $2 per week). This is meaningful as a mark of commitment to yourself and others, rather than a financial requirement. In return, you will learn ways to relate to the world more meaningfully. You will understand the value and rewards of practice. You will start attracting more love, peace, happiness and serenity in your life as you give the world those same gifts. This is the path to self-actualization and transcendence. There is no offer I can think of that is more rewarding.

*"If it is to be, it is up to me."*

—William Johnsen.

### *"Being For"*

By Dame Kim Conrad

"Are you for or against? We used to say...
Often, we did not know how else to get our way.

To live, to create, to manifest our dreams...
How we stood so strongly for, forced us against what we opposed, it seems.

Defining ourselves by what we are not
has cornered us in this convoluted spot.

When our Right is born by making others Wrong,
We dance for dominance all day long.

What if, while standing so passionately for
We embrace the contrast to meld in rapport.

Light does not live to be against the dark.
When the light is Being For, dark receives its part.

You may have day, I may have night, yet both exist continually
When you don't have to prove you're right.

We are coming to know all things are related
in this Wisdom where all are created.

Our left hand and right hand are opposite parts of a whole,
Yet the whole does not oppose itself – it houses our soul.

Mother Earth and All Relations are in this joint venture...
Release being self-indentured in Our adventure.

It's time, time to be valued opponents and amiable allies,
A blesséd tension that appeals to ascension.

Opposition is a creation of the mind.
Being opposite is a natural state, where reflection is refined.

Encountering differences, do you think: Your Thought – Or – Mine?
What if instead, they both could combine?

What if, a polarized world were a thing of the past
Now we have the ability to live Whole at last.

To live whole because we're starting to see
We are all part of Unity.

Miracles await us as we begin to soar
Flying past boundaries that estranged us before.

What if the cells of our body and us were to choose, simply choose
To live and be Heaven here at last,
So violence and imbalance are things of the past.

Cells changing the whole instead of the other way around.
Hmm...From all this deep awakening we live in Heaven Found.

So, Are you for or against? we used to say...
Now we can co-create our world in a magnificent way.

Holding your view while also seeing mine
Brings higher and deeper at the same time.

Uniting us Together in our timely rebirth,
Building this Garden of Heaven on Earth.

Summon Our Hearts – Remove all doubt.
Allow and Create Heaven All About."

Opposition is a creation of the mind.
Being opposite is a natural state, where reflection is refined.

Encountering differences, do you think: Your Thought – Or – Mine?
What if instead, they both could combine?

What if, a polarized world were a thing of the past
Now we have the ability to live Whole at last.

To live whole because we're starting to see
We are all part of Unity.

Miracles await us as we begin to soar
Flying past boundaries that estranged us before.

What if the cells of our body and us were to choose, simply choose
To live and be Heaven here at last,
So violence and imbalance are things of the past.

Cells changing the whole instead of the other way around.
Hmm...From all this deep awakening we live in Heaven Found.

So, Are you for or against? we used to say...
Now we can co-create our world in a magnificent way.

Holding your view while also seeing mine
Brings higher and deeper at the same time.

Uniting us Together in our timely rebirth,
Building this Garden of Heaven on Earth.

Summon Our Hearts – Remove all doubt.
Allow and Create Heaven All About."

https://kimconrad.com › being-for_291.html

# CHAPTER 2

# DEEP COMMUNITY

## THE RABBI'S GIFT

*M Scott Peck, Foundation for Community Encouragement,*
*A Different Drum*

The story of The Rabbi's Gift would be read at the beginning of the community group-building workshops conducted by the Foundation for Community Encouragement (FCE) in 1980s and 1990s, launched by the author and visionary M Scott Peck (*The Road Less Traveled*). It was another book by Dr. Peck, *The Different Drum,* that set me on a community-building path after a heart attack at age 42. This book launched a worldwide movement of FCE chapters. I attended two of these meetings, and they were transformative experiences. You can find links to the full story and the book at www.forthegoodofallnow.org.

## A Summary:

The story is about an old and dying monastic order consisting of an abbot and five monks. Over the years a rabbi would come on retreat to a small hut in the forest near the monastery, and the abbot and monks got to know him and sense when he was around. At a loss as to what he could do to save the order, the abbot visited the rabbi to ask him for advice. The rabbi could not offer much in terms of concrete advice: *"No, I am sorry,"* the rabbi responded. *"I have no advice to give. The only thing I can tell you is that the Messiah is one of you."*

The abbot and the monks pondered this advice over the next months, trying to decipher its meaning. As they did, they began to wonder if one of them was the Messiah. *"Suppose I am the Messiah? O God, not me."* The new insight, that one of them might be the Messiah, changed their behavior and they *"began to treat themselves with extraordinary respect."* The people who would come to the forest and visit the grounds and the old chapel, *"sensed this aura of extraordinary respect that now began to surround the five old monks and seemed to radiate out from them and permeate the atmosphere of the place."* They came more frequently and brought friends to this *"special place."*

As the young men engaged with the old monks, one of them asked if he could join the order, and soon others joined too. *"So, within a few years the monastery had once again become a thriving order and, thanks to the rabbi's gift, a vibrant center of light and spirituality in the realm."*

∞ ∞ ∞

# SECTION A: *Who am I? Who are We?*

## 1. Norms

Many of the traits that make human beings human are acquired behaviors. When acquired behaviors are adopted by a community of people, they establish the norms, customs, practices and cultural values of that community. Norms are not always necessarily good or healthy, but overall, they serve to improve the chances of survival and general wellbeing of the population. Norms, like cultures, are constantly changing and evolving hopefully for the better, but sometimes for the worse. This book will help you discern the difference. The rise of fascism globally, which is much in the news today, provides a timely example. The message is the same as the one that reverberated in Europe in the 1930s. Fascism is associated with Hitler and the Nazis, but it was introduced by Benito Mussolini in 1932 in Italy as "The Ideology of the Twentieth Century" calling for a state that would exercise *"full power and control."* The themes were hardly new, as fascism is just a different term for autocracy, tyranny, oppression, often connected to antisemitism and advocating violence as the means of ensuring "full power and control." These are not novel norms; rather, they are repetitive and end up as self-defeating because violence is simply unsustainable. "Remember that all through history, there have been tyrants and murderers, and for a time, they seem invincible. But in the end, they always fall. Always." Gandhi

The norms that shape our lives are sometimes referred to as institutions—a set of norms and values that describe the features of a society, typically including family, government, religion, education and the economy. For example, democracy and capitalism are institutions. Mary Oliver describes the effects of the institutions or norms that shape the current era: we crave power; love our 'stuff'; could care less about the wellbeing of nature and others; our politics and hearts are "small, and hard, and full of meanness." These Western norms have taken root globally. The Western norms and traditions gave birth to and often include democracy - the rule of the people. Democracy has established deep roots around the world, as roughly 50% of the world uses this system. Nevertheless, in many countries power is still vested in the hands of the few be they benevolent chiefs and leaders or dictators, autocrats, and tyrants. Democracy is certainly better than tyranny or fascism as it at least tries to be more egalitarian. Nonetheless, the institutions of capitalism and democracy have become weakened and corrupted. Lord Acton wrote in 1887 that "Power tends to corrupt, and absolute power corrupts absolutely." The corruption of democracy in the U.S. has disconnected the link between the governed (the people) and the governing classes (politicians, wealthy elites). The 'voice of the people' has been effectively suppressed in the corridors of power, where propaganda, money and power-*over* rule. This corruption of democracy was enshrined into law in the 2010 U.S. Supreme Court decision in Citizens United, which ignored precedent and reason and made the tortured argument that corporations had the same rights as people with respect to free speech. The floodgate of bribe money that has flowed since *absolutely* corrupted the already tattered foundation of democracy—the voice of the people. This silencing of the voice of the people is found regularly throughout history. The end of this saeculum is a mirror image of the end of the saeculum in the 1860s. The impotence of the Federal government to act on public safety, public health, inequality, and racism is not the result of random acts, but of a steady, deliberate corruption that seeks power-*over*. It is easy to think Mussolini may have been right about power and control, but we have an alternative and it was expressed by Gandhi, as I will describe later. Today, we are poised to take a major leap for humanity, which vision prevails—Gandhi's or Mussolini's—will be decided by the people, because the 'leaders' that brought us to this point are too weak and corrupt to tackle the enormous task that faces humanity now. The four critical points that will be made in For the Good of All, NOW! are:

1. Culture and norms are often contradictory, and they are constantly being influenced and changed.

2. All institutions act in their best interest.

3. Right relationship helps to ensure that power-*with* generates healthy, unifying norms, while power-*over* often generates unhealthy, divisive norms.

4. We have a choice. The alternative is staring us right in the face and it is very simple: Do good For the Good of All instead of Good for the Good of the Few.

> *"...Two roads diverged in a wood, and I, I took the one less traveled by, And that has made all the difference."*
> —"The Road Not Taken" by Robert Frost

## 2. Seeing with New Eyes

Gandhi's message, "Be the change you want to see in the world," is not too different from the rabbi's message and gift; both encourage us to find our inner sources of power. There is some doubt about whether Gandhi actually used those words, but he did state: "If we could change ourselves, the tendencies in the world would also change. As a man changes his own nature, so does the attitude of the world change towards him."

The secret for navigating toward *holos* is knowing that the 5 powers are already inside us: "The guest is inside you, and also inside me; you know the sprout is hidden inside the seed." When I begin to practice the 5 powers, I create a pulsation, a ripple of energy. When we act with the 5 powers, we create ripples that spread in ever-widening circles. Likewise, the rabbi did not tell the abbot that he needed to lead his order to a better place. The rabbi's gift was to give them a path to enter into symbiotic change—meaning change that comes from interdependency, arising from relationships that are mutually dependent and mutually beneficial. This is how the cosmos (spirit) and nature work. If you are willing to 'see with new eyes,' you will find the motivation and the power-*with* to step on this path, because this is not a solo crossing but a coming together of humankind. And it will make "all the difference."

## 3. Broken Social Compact & Fairness

*"Though force can protect in emergency, only justice, fairness, consideration and cooperation can finally lead men to the dawn of eternal peace."*

—Dwight D. Eisenhower

Although President, General Eisenhower was a warrior, he was also a man of principle in a time when principles mattered—at the beginning of the current saeculum. No matter what Eisenhower intended by using the word 'force,' power-*over* or power-*with*, it was clear that he understood the limitations of power-*over* and the enormous potential of power-*with*. He was clear that achieving an end nonviolently is much more powerful than achieving it violently. He warned the country that: "In the councils of government, we must guard against the acquisition of unwarranted influence, whether sought or unsought, by the military industrial complex. The potential for the disastrous rise of misplaced power exists and will persist." The military industrial complex has won that battle.

Even as the U.S. Congress is impotent to solve the crises of climate change, gun violence, the corruption of politics, racism, inequality, among many other failures, there is one thing they can agree on: funding and even over-funding the War Budget. To get a sense of how out of balance this is with the rest of the world, the U.S. spends more on defense than the *combined* defense budgets of China, India, Russia, the United Kingdom, Saudi Arabia, Germany, France, Japan, South Korea, Italy, and Australia. Why? Because, the American taxpayer is paying to maintain the *Pax Americana*, which doesn't really mean an American Peace, because America has been at war for most of the last 70 years, but rather the prevention of a third World War. The main beneficiary of the *Pax Americana* is 'free trade,' also known today as globalization. And who benefits most from globalization: corporations and the military industrial complex. The economic trade-off between military and social funding is known as the trade-off between 'guns and butter.' There is no question that, in the U.S., guns dominate over butter.

When the peasants ran out of bread during the French Revolution, Queen Marie Antoinette famously suggested, "Let them eat cake." This was not long before her head was chopped off. A revolution is coming. My hope, and one of the objectives of For the Good of All, NOW!, is to make sure that no heads are lost when the voice of the people is restored. There will be no need to tear down failing institutions. Let's simply build them up where they are needed, in our communities.

To put this in context, it seems there is little appetite in Washington DC to help the most disadvantaged—can't they just "eat cake"? While there is a gigantic appetite to ensure that capitalism flourishes globally, in America and the West generally, there used to be an argument that this produced good paying jobs until the capitalists shipped the jobs overseas. Since the 1980s' trickle-down economics of Ronald Reagan and Milton Friedman, the typical worker's take-home pay has been steadily declining. It certainly raised the extremely low pay rates in the 'under-developed' world, but it gutted the livelihoods of workers in the more advanced economies. Accounting for inflation, a typist making $4.10/hour in 1967 ought to be making $32.46/hour in 2021! (source: CNN). Would you like to guess where the $28.36 went? Between 1980 and 2020, the Gross Domestic Product rose 79%, the top 1% of earners received a 420% increase in their incomes, while the wages in the lower tier of workers rose only 20%. Trickle down, indeed!

The average wage for a crew member at McDonald's in the U.S. is $8.33, in Denmark the equivalent pay is $15. The cost of a hamburger is about the same in both countries. Every citizen in Denmark has access to *free* health care services. In America, people pay vastly more for health care than in any other industrialized country in the world. Medical bankruptcy is not uncommon in the so-called richest nation on earth.

Most Americans who go on to postsecondary education amass huge debt loads. In Europe these burdens are shared amongst the taxpayers, including having the wealthy and corporations pay a fair share. In the U.S., it costs more for daycare than many take home in wages. So, what does this all say about our priorities in the U.S.? It tells us that our social compact is unfair and broken, that it has been for some time, and that it will not get better from the top down.

**Rebuilding the social compact can and will <u>only</u> get done from the bottom up.**

Fairness is something all humans can appreciate as part of their relationship with other human beings. It is rarely mentioned in terms of our relationship with nature, but it should be. At its simplest, fairness means everyone is entitled to share in the bounty and the sacrifice—an *equal opportunity of benefits and costs.* Furthermore, fairness implies sharing the rewards of a given effort to the benefits received in return—a *proportional distribution of benefits and costs* (more on these two topics later). Finally, fairness is an expression of compassion—walk a mile in the other person's shoes, as the old saying goes.

**Right relationship to each other means caring about and being fair to each other.**

## 4. On Value and Values

In 2006 I met Douglas K. Smith at a training sponsored by the United Way Of America centered on his book: *On Value and Values—Thinking Differently about We...in An Age of Me.* We quickly formed a strong bond. I credit both Joanna Macy and Doug for introducing me to the power-*over* and power-*with* insights, while Doug profoundly re-shaped my understanding of how communities and organizations work. As you read the following additional insights from *On Value and Values,* think of them as signs you can look for to sharpen your instincts. As Einstein cautioned: "We cannot solve our problems with the same level of thinking that created them."

*Shared Values* are the "beliefs, behaviors, attitudes, and speech regarding social, political, economic, family, religious, technological, environmental, and other matters. They are strong when predictable, regardless of whether they are considered good or bad." Shared Values are created by Thick *We's* who *share a common fate*. In this context, *shared fates* are real and obvious, going much deeper than the fates of being born and dying that we share with 8 billion people on earth. Rather, *shared fates* are "the inescapable, tangible, and everyday sense that one's interests and purposes depend on other people." Thick *We's* are created where people "must implement the common good together because they share fates" like in communities of the past where our health and safety depended on each other. Doug Smith recognized the difference between the pursuit of the *Greater Good*—"Any number of interests or purposes that might define or measure happiness in large social formations, such as markets, networks, and nations." and the *Common Good*, the Good of All, which is created through the "shared purposes and shared values of a Thick *We*"- people with whom we, tangibly, share fates. His conclusion was that the strong *shared purposes* of organizations *could be* harnessed to do more than create the *Greater Good,* they could be repurposed to create the *Common Good*—wellbeing, the Good of All.

**The unlimited pursuit of the Greater Good for the Few will soon be replaced by the shared objective of the Good For All at all levels of human society.**

In reality, organizations are created to pursue whatever delivers the organization its greatest good, and only a few ever achieved the leap to generate the common good. In healthy self-organizing systems, like the complex immune systems that protect us from disease, there is a constant feedback loop of information and data that is essential to the whole body. The transmission of this cellular information-sharing is *holistic*—the cells are the system, and the system are the cells. This is both a feature of and an essential ingredient to the living functionality of the system. Self-organizing systems must also be able to distinguish from all the feedback what is in the best interest of the whole—the common good. This is complicated and requires agile and rapid feedback loops to test and refine good feedback from not so good feedback. In hierarchies, the process is slower and more rigid. Feedback and information have to pass through layers to get to a level where a decision can be made and passed back down the layers to be implemented. The more important the decision, the more layers of authority it travels through. At each layer power-*over* increases. The power-*with* of egalitarian societies or natural systems are much quicker and more nimble and can process more information than anything man has ever been able to duplicate and on a scale that is almost impossible to imagine.

"People who promote value without values hollow out and sicken the individual and group souls."

—Doug Smith

"All the resources we will need arise out of our interactions, as we commit ourselves to a common intent for our common fate."
—Joanna Macy

"At Patagonia, we appreciate that all life on earth is under threat of extinction. We're using the resources we have—our business, our investments, our voice and our imaginations—to do something about it." The outdoor apparel company, Patagonia. It would be remiss not to mention that cooperatives and employee-owned enterprises are joined by the new community benefit corporations at the vanguard of this new wave of caretaker organizations.

*The fate and happiness of human society depends on people committing to use their voices, imaginations, wisdom and resources to do good For the Good of All, NOW!*

# SECTION B: *Where are We going?*

Already, we can view the future through the different lenses presented in the first half of this book. I want you to challenge my assumptions and projections, because I want you to think about the path ahead.

One of the purposes of this book is to prompt readers to think about the future critically. Sit quietly and focus on what you want to become and how you want to live in relationship to the world. If you think the future I describe is misguided, why? What do you envision will happen? The following three categories may serve as a good start:

## 1. Time is Marching On

Time only cycles forward. The following 6 points all lead to a major shift: (1) the *cycles of history* (The Fourth Turning), (2) the *long sweep of history* (Macroshift), which will mark major changes in humanity's relationship to each other and our environment, (3) the growing *spiritual perception* of The Great Turning, (4) the advanced stages of a planetary climate system in *chaos* and subject to even minor fluctuations, (5) the rise of *cultural and evolutionary signals* (fascism; emergence of Prosocial World), even (6) the popularity of *'holism' in modern vocabulary*. This is not the first major civilizational, cultural, social, and institutional break with the past, nor is it likely to be the last, in my opinion. If there are compelling arguments that we are just going through a bad period and everything will get back to normal soon, let them be heard. One argument that will not hold water is that somehow humans are not subject to the laws of nature, physics, and time. The more people have turned their attention even briefly towards this great confluence—coming together—of events, the easier it is to see with new eyes. Listen to Kabir "Let your arrogance go, and look around inside." It is time to engage.

## 2. Climate Change Is Getting Worse

Climate Change is *the* most significant factor relating to any analysis of what our future will look like. The permafrost, the land mass surrounding the North Pole, has been thawing. This thaw will cause a rapid doubling of the greenhouse effect. Meanwhile, in the Arctic in the summer of 2020 temperatures were 10° C (50°F) above average. In March of 2022, weather stations in East Antarctica were close to 30° Celsius (54° Fahrenheit) above average for this time of the year (https://weather.co/). At the Concordia weather station, the temperature reached 50° C (90° F) above average! Think about this for a moment. What would happen if the temperature rose to this level where you live even for a relatively short period? For most of the world, even if it was just a few days, the loss of habitat and life, human and animal, would be shocking. For reference, at 40°C (105°F), outdoor activity is dangerous and limited to a few hours at most.

The temperature rise in the Antarctic and across the permafrost is more than a little fluctuation. We know that even minor fluctuations in chaotic complex systems have outsized effects (the butterfly effect). Even if our 'leaders' continue their endless and fruitless debates about who is going to do what about it, you and I don't have to. Billions of people have been active in reducing climate damage by demanding the 'leaders' do something about this existential threat, and they have succeeded in slowing the rate at which the greenhouse effect was growing. Even if it continues to grow, we can be grateful for this herculean effort. But it really shouldn't be this hard! The current power-*over* system has vested power in the hands of 'leaders' who are beholden to their own interests—to amass wealth, to retain political power, to hold tightly onto their power-*over*. It is not realistic to think that they will decide to suddenly rein in the systems that have given them so much power. The only way real change will come, is when *We the People* take back the reins and exert our power-*with* in our communities, making change from the bottom up, and letting it spread holistically, naturally to create good for the Good of All, NOW! and for future generations What are you for?

## 3. Fear

Fear is a powerful motivator. It is an instinctual reaction that can prevent injury and save life. It can also be an impediment when it prevents you from doing something that ultimately is in your best interest. As I see it there are two fears at play in the context of the coming macroshift: the fear of instability and the fear of loss. The fear of the loss of culture is why there are still fundamentalists in this world hanging on to a past that will never come back, and it is what drives people to try to hang on to a past that is changing too fast for them. Fear of loss will always use power-*over* to achieve its aims of maintaining its belief systems. Fear of pain and suffering, be it physical or emotional—such as social disapproval or fear of embarrassment—also urges us to bury our heads in the sand. This is why it is so important to develop the awareness that when we let go of the fear of suffering, we become empowered. The practice of Circle will empower you to take back the reins using power-*with*. Together, aware of our shared fates, we are empowered to co-create the values that result in the common good.

## 4. Instability

The war in Ukraine is destabilizing capitalism, geo-political relationships, and globalization, all for the sake of reclaiming the glorified past of the Soviet Union and Tsarist Russia. In 1905 George Santayana wrote, "Those who cannot remember the past are condemned to repeat it." If you are trying to make sense of the future, you have to consider the possibility that the destabilizing effect of war creates its own whirlpool, sucking in ever more violence and producing ever more chaos. It is either naïve or wishful thinking to think the chaos of this ill-fated war can be tamed. Violence begets more violence, until it collapses of its own weight. History tells us that peace only comes when all other solutions are exhausted. The historic parallels point to this war evolving into a larger conflict, even nuclear war, all directly or indirectly related to the war in Ukraine. This is the nature of chaos. Instability, whether from a pandemic, a war (especially involving a nuclear power), or climate change will result in destabilizing globalization. Deglobalization will have wide-reaching consequences for the world and humankind. War is the ultimate use of power-*over*. It can only be defeated as a result of its own collapse or by the force of power-*with*. The ultimate solution to war, is not more violence, it is peace. "When will they ever learn?" (*Where Have All the Flowers Gone,* Peter, Paul and Mary, lyrics by Pete Seeger.)

## 5. *'A Grand Solution'?*

Strauss and Howe's research indicates that "come the Fourth Turning, in the white heat of society's... rebirth, a grand solution may suddenly snap into place." No one can tell for sure whether or if such a miraculous rebirth will arise, but the end of the chaos will be dependent on our individual and collective willingness to become agents of change. I think the transition will be challenging and slower to materialize in Western cultures than in the cultures with stronger links to their indigenous pasts and beliefs in essential oneness. There have only been three other *macroshifts* in the history of mankind. None provide a roadmap for the current era, but we are still here on Earth, and we've successfully navigated three of these huge changes before, so the track record is promising. Those who came before us faced major challenges with fewer tools and assets. We can only hope that we follow in their footsteps by choosing the path "less traveled by" (Robert Frost). A grand solution will not turn back the clock, rather it is most likely to usher in a new era of *globalism*—expressed as the many interconnections that create One Planet—One People—which is quite different from *globalization*, which describes most frequently economic relationships and global markets, but also includes political and cultural trends.

## 6. True Community

Peck's four-step path to "True Community" most assuredly contains wisdom for all of us. The rabbi breathes new life into an old monastic order by planting the seeds of potentiality in their minds. Kabir called potentiality "the sprout...hidden inside the seed." The following steps reflect the path it takes to get to *True Community.*

a. **Pseudocommunity**: members are overtly pleasant to each other and avoid conflict; while differences are papered over, the group appears to be cohesive.

b. **Chaos**: starts as soon as members of the group express their differences; attempts to heal, convert, suppress, and organize a way out (electing a leader, for example) will disrupt the attainment of "true community." (Leadership is a co-responsibility shared by everyone.)

c. **Emptiness**: the path out of chaos is the toughest challenge for most people, it requires emptying selfhood—preconceptions, prejudices, expectations, ideologies—and resisting the need to fix others. The first step on this path occurs when a person begins to speak their joy or empty themselves of their sorrows. In group practice or in any respectful setting this can become a highly packed emotional moment during which the discipline of holding peace and listening deeply, rather than reacting, is critical. A common insight coming from this experience is the realization that we are all broken and suffering in some way.

d.  **True Community**: out of the darkness of the innermost fears
we all have, the group begins the process of healing. The
entire group moves into centeredness and calmness in unity
and peace. Listening from the heart and with spirit.

The practice of Circle will reflect these four stages. Circle is the
portal to compassion for others and for yourself. In Circle, we learn to
embrace suffering—our own and the suffering of others. We don't try
to fix suffering. We accept it for ourselves and for others. When strong
emotions arise, a space opens up to hold this tension. Keeping your
peace, listening to your heart, hearing fully and compassionately, this
is the practice that provides you with the awareness necessary to cope
with chaos. Whether in Circle or in life, when chaos swirls around you,
your Circle practice will help you to restore peace through awareness,
mindfulness and insight. It is in this space that you will practice the Four
Truths: "Suffering is part of what it means to be human. When we resist
change, we suffer. Suffering ends when we let go and stop resisting. From
birth to death, our actions and ultimate goal are to realize our essential
oneness." This is incredibly powerful: the path to oneness, which is the
destination of the *holos* macroshift, lies in this awareness. This is a life-
altering experience for those going through the process the first time.
The practice of Circle means you get to drink from this cup safely, in the
shelter of each other, as often as necessary.

At the end of the three-day FCE Circle, I felt still and in communion—
empowered not necessarily as an individual, as much as a member of
the now much smaller remaining Circle. I imagined vividly, as if I was
observing a scene in which I was a participant, that if someone entered
the Circle and challenged us to solve the most stubborn problem facing
humankind, we would have been able to solve the challenge. As I conjure
up that transformative moment, I step into that scene and relive the
feeling as if it were happening now, rather than thirty years ago! But with
a significant twist, today I understand that our mission would *not* be to

solve the challenge, rather it would be to empower the seekers in our midst to find their path. This is the power of the rabbi's wisdom. This is the power of the Hero's Journey. It is always about finding the answer for yourself. It is always facilitated by special companions. It always asks you to let go.

> *"The Guest is inside you, and also inside me;*
> *you know the sprout is hidden inside the seed.*
> *We are all struggling; none of us has gone far.*
> *Let your arrogance go, and look around inside."*
> —Kabir

This is the lasting gift: find your self-belief in the practice of Circle and you will find true community. Find true community and you will change the world.

## 7. Self-Rule—The Power of Community

Humans are now confronted with the greatest evolutionary challenge since we came down from the trees and started our journey toward the dominant species we are today. We are forced to consider a stark choice as a species: adapt or perish. This is a crisis of *our* own making. Fortunately for us, Mahatma Gandhi has already designed a system of governance for the *holistic* paradigm called *Swaraj*—literally self-rule—based on his understanding that nature was in essence cooperative rather than competitive. Gandhi's three-part Vision For The World still stands: Coexist nonviolently and peacefully. Vest power in the individual. Seek the highest common good—the Good of All.

The basis for nonviolence is what Gandhi called Spirit Force and Martin Luther King, Jr. called love force':

> **"Love is the only force capable of transforming an enemy**
> **into a friend."**

Gandhi's vision was based on the ancient tribal and village systems of India and similar to those evident throughout the long history of the rise of Homo *sapiens*. The natural leaders and caretakers of a village— which might have included elders, business, and civic association leaders, among others—would be chosen by the villagers. These leaders would meet in a Circle, which Gandhi called a People's Committee. The Circle would meet in the public square, the outer participants listening to the discussion of the Circle and invited to participate. However, politicians and political party activities were expressly excluded. The ultimate agreement would be acclaimed by consensus by the whole village. The village circle would elect representatives to ever-widening geographic circles of People's Committees. The community would thus be connected in a hive-like structure that fostered information sharing and feedback loops and created a process for self-rule. Gandhi projected that the center of power would shift from the political parties, and their representatives, to consensual democracy, the voice of the people.

*Self-rule* and the Political Committees movement suffered two setbacks: Gandhi's assassination shortly after launching the movement in the 1940s; and after a highly successful revival in 1960s and 70s by Jayprakash Narayan, who succumbed "for the sake of India" to allow its participants to join the Janata party and participate in a critical electoral defeat of the autocratic Indira Gandhi. The movement had been growing rapidly until then because people loved it, but its politicization marked its second early downfall.

I learned this history from two papers written over twenty years ago by Terry Mollner, one of the pioneers of socially responsible investing and founder of the Trusteeship Institute, Common Good Capitalism, and a founding member of the Calvert Social Investment Fund. Narayan, before he died, would make it clear to Mr. Mollner that he regretted the decision to allow the movement to be politicized. This is a strong warning that *For the Good of All, NOW!* must *never* become politicized. It is a movement of the people and by the people.

> **Consensual democracy will peacefully replace the systems where political parties compete against each other. Our system of governance will move from power-over to power-with.**

Margaret Mead is right, real leadership comes from the bottom up, not the top down. It is time for people to advocate for change in their communities. It is time for *We the People* to organize at the community level and demand better. Demand that the wellbeing of all, the common good, be the Prime Directive in your community. Demand self-rule in your community. The voice of the people can only come from people who share fates and values. This means people need to rekindle their sense of community. This would normally be a tall order in the era of the cult of individualism, but the coming chaos will soon make Thick *We*'s out of most of us. It will also prompt at the individual level a much deeper craving for deep relationships that go beyond pseudo-community. Circle will become the defining characteristic of human relationship, inserting itself back where it used to be, as part of the first tier of social relationships beyond immediate family, and a critical part of kinship, tribe, and community.

When *We the People* organize to produce community shared wisdom to describe how we want to live together in unity and peace and strive to do good for the good of all, and when we circulate this shared wisdom through a bustling interconnected hive of communities, the voice of the people, the voice of power-*with* will rise above the din of the 'leaders' and elites who seek to assert power-*over*. Where we lead, they will follow. Remember, "Never doubt that a small group of thoughtful, committed citizens can change the world indeed, it's the only thing that ever has." Margaret Mead

## 8. PROSOCIAL WORLD—New Evolutionary Technology

*"Large-scale human society cannot be built directly from individuals.*
*It needs to be multicellular, like a multicellular organism. Individuals*
*need to function within small groups, which in turn need to be*
*organized into larger groups such as cities, which in turn need to*
*be organized into still larger groups such as states, nations and the*
*global village. Empowering the small groups was just as important*
*as, indeed a prerequisite for, empowering the large ones."*

The Neighborhood Project—Using Evolution to Improve My City,
One Block at a Time" (2011) David Sloan Wilson.

I consider meeting David Sloan Wilson another set of many *non-*coincidences in my life that provided me with the building blocks that For the Good of All, NOW! describes. The groundbreaking Prosocial technologies will connect the dots of *personal* transformation to *societal* transformation and adaptation, as part of an evolutionary model.

Thanks to the collaboration of Nobelist Elinor Ostrum (*Governing the Commons,* 1990) and evolutionary biologist David Sloan Wilson, we discover, just in time, that the keys to organize and manage human activity effectively were hiding in plain sight. Their combined effort laid bare a longstanding misconception called "The Tragedy of the Commons" (Garret Hardin 1968) which gave rise to the shared belief that humans would inevitably seek personal gain over the good of the group. Hardin's famous essay proposed that a group of herders who agreed to manage a common meadow would, as a result of personal ambition or need, inevitably seek to take advantage over the others by 'freeloading'— taking more than the agreed upon share —while contributing the same as everyone else to the maintenance costs. Commons have existed since humans started settling down along riverbanks and cultivating the land. The commons is simply a shared resource that is communally governed for the benefit of all the *commoners* it serves.

Those who live and tend the commons are referred to as Commoners. Ostrum's research found many examples where the commons had been successfully managed for years, thousands of years in some cases, for the benefit of all (water-sharing, fisheries, high alpine meadows). The gift she gave the world consisted of cataloging eight principles to successfully govern the commons thus refuting the commonly held belief that Hardin described. ("Governing the Commons: The Evolution of Institutions for Collective Action," Elinor Ostrum, 2009 Nobel Prize Winner.)

David Sloan Wilson immediately grasped that Ostrum's eight principles had evolutionary scale implications connected to his work. David and Lin Ostrum collaborated on the formulation of these principles as "The 8 Core Design Principles" for all groups and organizations, thus creating a basis for self-management of *prosocial* societies. This is a monumental evolutionary tool! It is a quite literally a new operating manual that will allow small groups and entire societies to govern themselves. I urge you to pause a second in your reading to let the previous sentence sink in. The implications of this research are based on numerous real-world successful examples of human cooperation, and they are captured in a new movement called Prosocial World. *"Prosocial World developed the first change method based on evolutionary science that enhances cooperation & collaboration for groups of all types & sizes and is effective at a global scale."* (https://www.prosocial.world/) The quest to achieve a more fair and equitable world now has a set of governing principles that, if followed, would work to achieve the good of all, not just for humans, but for humans and nature!

### *Prosocial principles are valid for all kinds of groups—institutions, organizations, governments, small and large groups.*

Businesses that Doug Smith perceived as capable of creating values as well as value can now be managed successfully to produce social values as well as economic value for the common good. For the Good of All, NOW! circles mean that *We the People* have a *True Community* voice in a way that Gandhi had imagined, only now much more interconnected and instantaneous. The significant impacts from climate change, the collapse of globalization, nations, capitalism, all of which have used power-*over* to freeload for the benefit of the 'leaders' and elites, is about to collapse of its own weight. This chaos will also reignite our sense of shared fates leading to the Thick *We*'s who will forge the new customs, values and norms of the emerging paradigm of *holos*.

The center of power-*with* will be local and it will be holistic, sweeping away hierarchies that impede efficiency and create imbalance. Nature is the most efficient, most complex system we can imagine. Its design relies on subsidiarity—the bottom affects the top. You and I can and do affect all of humanity because subsidiarity is a natural force. In hierarchies the few can reign over the many through power-*over*. This is unnatural which is why it is inefficient and results in tragedy. In the very near future, it will be natural for us to use the same structure and interconnection that nature has created. I know this seems ridiculously simplistic. But that is the beauty of self-rule. It is really this simple:

**We are the fulcrum. *Circle* is the lever, and
The 8 Core Design Principles are the operating system.**

### The 8 Core Design Principles (CDPs)

CDP1: Shared identity and purpose
CDP2: Equitable distribution of contributions and benefits
CDP3: Fair and inclusive decision-making
CDP4: Monitoring of agreed behaviors
CDP5: Graduated responding to helpful and unhelpful behavior
CDP6: Fast and fair conflict resolution
CDP7: Authority to self-govern (according to principles 1-6)
CDP8: Collaborative relations with other groups (using principles 1-7)

**These eight principles are relevant to *every organization and group*—government, business, religious, community, and Circle.**

To explore this topic further go to https://www.prosocial.world/. You will readily appreciate how these eight principles fit with Circle practices. For the Good of All, NOW! is currently working with Prosocial World, as David and his team roll out a major initiative to stimulate the formation of prosocial groups. There will be opportunities for Circle participants to connect directly and indirectly with Prosocial World. For a fuller understanding of this world-changing technology I encourage you to connect through our site to theirs. I would encourage every Circle to participate in a basic training course for your Circle. It is a powerful technology.

This model, when applied with a process called Acceptance and Commitment Therapy or ACT—which sounds a lot more complicated than it is—helps groups define a course of action and then commit to implementing it as a group. You will learn how to strengthen your Circle with ACT training. Developed as a therapy, this model is a powerful tool that works quickly and highly effectively to supercharge the effectiveness of groups. It is simple, intuitive, and compatible with the practice of Circle and with the Five Powers, especially mindfulness. For anyone trying to maximize the experience of Circle in their daily lives and communities, the benefits of even 15 minutes of applying the ACT matrix are experienced immediately and will persist for some time. If you are trying to do good For the Good of All incorporating prosocial technology in your Circle practice will anchor these new behaviors and states of mind for the long term.

Prosocial connects the dots from the power of Circle to the power of community. It is simple to understand, and it is the operating technology for self-rule today, as well as for the future paradigm. It will also change how organizations thrive and survive in the new era. Already, there is plenty of evidence of this in the rise of popularity of localism and cooperative businesses and the growing importance and spread of Community Benefit Corporations (CBCs) and B Corp certification.

# SECTION C: *How are We getting there?*

## 1. Practice and Mindfulness

The second power, diligence, is the power of practice. A personal practice that will align your life with your power-*with*. It is nothing short of life changing.

The rabbi did not give the monks new wisdom and insight, he set them on a path to find their own wisdom and insight. The wisdom was always in them. The rabbi's message led them to reconnect to their power-*with*. As they became more compassionate towards each other, they saw each other through new eyes. They tapped into the first power—self-belief. They were well acquainted with the second power, diligence, also known as a practice, because monks practice a lot. The third power—mindfulness—was experienced in the little pause, 'what if he is the Messiah?' that each monk would ask himself and which erased the old assumptions they held about each other. Soon they began to 'treat each other with extraordinary respect.' What a difference that split second of mindfulness makes!

*"There's something happening here. What it is ain't exactly clear...a man with a gun over there telling me I got to beware...Nobody's right if everybody's wrong"* are some of the lyrics of a popular song by the group Buffalo Springfield in 1967. As it came to be proved in the Pentagon Papers, the U.S. government out-and-out lied to the American people about the reasons for and mismanagement of the Vietnam war. People understood the war to be wrong, yet the government persisted and violently suppressed anti-war activity. Are the governments of the world

lying to us now about the extent of the cataclysm facing all humanity? Yes, they certainly are. Do they show any signs of trying to limit the insane pursuit of growth for the benefit of the few, also known as greed? No. In the most charitable interpretation, the 'emerging' economies believe that they have a right to continue polluting because they didn't contribute as much to pollution as the advanced economies. The advanced economies claim everybody has to share in the pain equally. *Both are wrong.* Growth is killing us all NOW. The international institutions which grew out of the *Pax Americana*—the United Nations, the World Bank, the IMF, the World Health Organization, NATO, the International Criminal Court, the EU, global price-setting (markets), etc.—are essentially willing participants in a world where power-*over* is concentrated in the hands of a few who hold most of the power and money.

In *A Tale of Two Cities* (1859), Charles Dickens' story set in London and Paris during the French Revolution (1789-1799), Dickens could have been describing our current time: *"It was the best of times, it was the worst of times, it was the age of wisdom, it was the age of foolishness, it was the epoch of belief, it was the epoch of incredulity, it was the season of light, it was the season of darkness, it was the spring of hope, it was the winter of despair."* Although Dickens wrote this in 1859 describing the overthrow of the royalty in France one hundred years earlier, during the same period that witnessed the birth of nationalism, capitalism and the creation of the U.S., this description fits the moment of great transition we are in perfectly: *"the spring of hope"* and *"the winter of despair."* Hope is not a strategy, but it *is* a powerful force for action. Hope flowed from the rabbi's gift. It was accessed through moments of mindfulness.

## 2. Diligence and Mindfulness—Practice and Slowing Down

Having the *Diligence* to maintain a regular practice is challenging for many of us. When you set aside a specific time to *practice* slowing down, Thich Nhat Hanh provides four directions: 1) avoid negative thoughts, energy; 2) replace negative energy with positive energy—accept and release; 3) invite positive 'seeds'—a line of poetry or a memory; 4) try to hold those seeds in your awareness as long as possible. You can slow down almost anywhere anytime through the *practice* of deep breathing, relaxing and allowing your belly to rise and fall with each breath. Even a few minutes of this simple exercise of slowing down can help you to realign and regenerate your energy throughout the day. As you observe that the practice brings you peace and serenity, it becomes empowering. Monks seclude themselves in a monastery, because it is difficult to maintain a practice steadily without the support of others. We can duplicate this in our lives, every night as a practice to bring on sleep and whenever concentration is needed and in Circle.

**Mindfulness** is the art of being *present*, being aware of what is happening right NOW! The more you practice it the better you'll get at it. Deepak Chopra, in *The Seven Spiritual Laws of Success,* compared our busy lives to an out-of-control stagecoach. He urged us to conjure up this image while realizing you are in the driver's seat. You have the agency to pull on the reins. No one is stopping you from exercising that agency, but you. Slow down. Pause. Breathe deeply. Clear your mind and observe your thoughts. If you have never done this, you will quickly realize what Chopra described. Let the thoughts come and let them go. Don't worry. Don't dwell. Just let go. The stagecoach will slow down.

## The Shambhala Prophecy

"Coming to us across twelve centuries, the prophecy about the coming of the Shambhala warriors illustrates the challenges we face in our time." Joanna Macy learned it in 1980 from her friend and teacher Choegyal Rinpoche of the Tashi Jong community in northern India.

There comes a time when all life on Earth is in danger. In this era, great barbarian powers have arisen. Although these powers spend their wealth in preparations to annihilate one another, they have much in common: weapons of unfathomable destructive power, and technologies that lay waste to our world. In this era, when the future of sentient life hangs by the frailest of threads, the kingdom of Shambhala emerges.

You cannot go there, for it is not a place; it is not a geopolitical entity. It exists in the hearts and minds of the Shambhala warriors— that is the term Choegyal used, "warriors." Nor can you recognize a Shambhala warrior when you see her or him, for they wear no uniform or insignia, and they carry no banners. And there are no barricades on which to climb to threaten the enemy, or behind which they can hide to rest or regroup. They do not even have any home turf. Always they must move on the terrain of the barbarians themselves.

Now the time comes when great courage—moral and physical courage—is required of the Shambhala warriors, for they must go into the very heart of the barbarian power, into the pits and pockets and citadels where the weapons are kept, to dismantle them. To dismantle the weapons, in every sense of the word, they must go into the corridors of power where the decisions are made.

The Shambhala warriors have the courage to do this because the weapons are *manomaya* "mind-made.Made by the human mind, they can be unmade by the human mind. The Shambhala warriors know that the dangers threatening life on Earth are not visited upon us by any extraterrestrial power, satanic deities, or preordained evil fate. They arise from our own decisions, our own lifestyles, and our own relationships.

So, in this time, the Shambhala warriors go into training. When Choegyal said this, Joanna asked, "How do they train?" They train, he said, in the use of two weapons. "What weapons?" And he held up his hands the way the lamas hold the ritual objects of dorje and bell, in the lama dance. The weapons are compassion and insight. Both are necessary, he said. You have to have compassion because it gives you the juice, the power, the passion to move. It means not to be afraid of the pain of the world. Then you can open to it, step forward, act. But that weapon by itself is not enough. It can burn you out, so you need the other—you need insight into the radical interdependence of all phenomena. With that wisdom you know that it is not a battle between good guys and bad guys, but that the line between good and evil runs through the landscape of every human heart. With insight into our profound interrelatedness— our deep ecology—you know that actions undertaken with pure intent have repercussions throughout the web of life, beyond what you can measure or discern. By itself, that insight may appear too cool, too conceptual, to sustain you and keep you moving, so you need the heat of compassion. Together these two can sustain us as agents of wholesome change. They are gifts for us to claim now in the healing of our world."

Abstracted from: *Coming Back to Life,*
*World as Self World as Lover,* Joanna Macy.

The Kingdom of Shambhala, as described in this 1200-year-old prophecy is rising NOW throughout the world. Its emissaries (a more modern word and perhaps more precise than warrior) are training to gain the powers of wisdom and insight. The emissaries arise in response to the imminent threats of extinction. They are ordinary people. They don't just gather on social media, or march in the streets, or occupy the public squares, they enter the corridors of power in their communities. They gather in the ancient practice of Circle, to build the powers of compassion and insight, and develop shared wisdom to do good For the Good of All. The more the self-inflicted chaos rains down suffering on the people of the earth, the bigger the Kingdom of Shambhala grows. In ever-widening Circles, the curtains of deception and greed are pulled back to expose the truth: Good for the Good of the Few is not a good way to run any system. More and more of us choose *"Being For"* by reconnecting to the radical universal interbeing of nature's oneness by vesting power in the individual, coexisting peacefully and nonviolently, and by seeking good For the Good of All. I encourage you to print and re-read *"Being For"*. As you do, you will replace the old antisocial out-of-date operating manual for humanity and replace it with the new holistic paradigm. In the Kingdom of Shambhala on Earth, humanity's insight transcends the limitations of the power-*over* patterns of humanity's adolescence to become the fully adult power-*with* beings we were destined to be—physically, spiritually, and energetically interconnected as One.

## 3. The Ancient Practice of Circle

The *practice* of Circle teaches you how to be *mindful*. In Circle, we hear joy and suffering and then internalize it, mull it over, feeling each other's joy or pain. The less we talk the more chance we have to be present. It takes a little practice to learn how to do this, but when you do, it is life-changing for you and for those around you. Declan Coyle, the Irish public speaker, author, and trainer, tells a beautiful story about making breakfast with his daughter. She insists on carrying the eggs from the refrigerator to the counter and she drops them. His immediate reaction is anger, but the pained and fearful look on her face causes him to pause. In that split second, he chooses a different response—instead of—*Now look what you've done. Clean up your mess*—anger and power-*over*; he chooses compassion, loving-kindness and power-*with*—*Oh dear, let's get this cleaned up together*. Imagine yourself in this scenario as the father, then as the daughter. Imagine the impact of the different responses. Do you see the power of mindfulness and how simple it can be to develop this skill? I hope you can actually sense the difference. Circle is made for developing mindfulness. It is where you become *mindful of your power to choose* how to *be* in the world. It costs nothing, but instead of draining your energy, it adds *positive energy*. Practicing mindfulness becomes second nature, popping up in your consciousness when you need it most, in moments of stress or happiness. Mindfulness is acquired through practice.

Circle is the perfect platform for learning and practicing the power-keys that I share with you here. Every one of them is much more easily attained through the additional power of Circle, which shifts your world as you sense *'this aura of extraordinary respect that... seemed to radiate out...and permeate the atmosphere of the place.'* The power of self-belief and the power of practice are life-changing for you and for the world. Developing the skills to recognize and be mindful of how you use these powers is very difficult to do alone. In the shelter of each other in Circle, your *compassion* expands and with it happiness and serenity expand in your *"aura,"* and you become, like our friends in the Rabbi's Gift: *"a vibrant center of light and spirituality."* The practice of Circle builds with every circle encounter.

While others busy themselves building sea walls, weapons of mass destruction, space tourism, and engaging in war, let us rebuild our communities in the shelter of each other through the simple and ancient practice of Circle. We introduce Circle technology here to those who are not familiar with this practice, which I contend is one of the most important technologies humans ever invented and astonishingly well designed to work with the eight Core Design Principles. Christina Baldwin's *Calling the Circle* describes its origins: *"The circle is a common first culture that is indigenous to all peoples, including the white tribes of pre-Roman Europe. Campfire rings in Africa and the Nile Delta date back more than 100,000 years."*

The practice of Circle shifts a typical conversation to a *"discussion in a receptive attitude of thoughtful speaking and deep listening."* Another good resource for Circle practice comes from Parker Palmer's Circle of Trust® strategies. There are many more, but they all link back to the safe space that is essential to the ancient practice of circle. Julie Krull,

Kurt Johnson, and Deborah Moldow are additional resources. (See the Resources section for links to these people and their organizations and The Circle Way's Guidelines at www.forthegoodofallnow.org.)

Circle is not a strange cult. It is a practice that is found in almost every culture. We come to Circle to listen, to quieten our minds and listen to our heart and spirit. We speak only when moved to do so. Often there is a 'talking piece' that is passed to a person who wishes to speak. Rather than the typical statement followed by response, there is silence to allow each person to reflect on what has been spoken. There is no need to respond until and unless you are moved to do so. Speak when you are moved to speak. This is all about listening to your inner voice and being authentic, loving, and sincere. There will be lots of quiet space. Do not feel compelled to fill it. You are communicating silently with each other through your thoughts and spirit. You focus your awareness on what you are hearing and internalizing it, not formulating a response! Circle is where you will find both deep meaningful connection and the superpower of *Deep Community*. It is a practice that will connect your power-*with* to the power-*with* of others, your spirit with the spirit of others, your love with the love of others. Learning how to <u>be</u> brings about how to <u>become</u>. **Circle is a Superpower**.

The simple practices of Circle are intuitive once you've done them a few times. They are life-changing when you practice them diligently. You will soon notice the difference in your daily life. The more you notice, the more it becomes second nature. Circle is the safe space that allows for surrender. Out of that surrender comes the great power of power-*with*. And then in the shelter of each other we rise together, achieving the most prized of all human states—actualizing the full potential of our humanity and essential oneness. In every aspect of your life, you will find that you are capable of performing better as long as you remain in right relationship with the world.

## 4. Calling the Circle

Circles come in all kinds of types and for all sorts of purposes. For the Good of All, NOW! specifically refers to the circle practice we embrace as Shared wisdom Circles, but any existing Circle can sign up if you agree to the basics of membership (see below). For the Good of All, NOW! will connect participants through the website and through a 'hive' that will coalesce and instantaneously connect all Shared Wisdom Circles. There is more downloadable information, links, and training materials than this book will permit at www.forthegoodofallnow.org.

Circle is not the space where a person comes to heal conditions that require professional help. But, in the search for meaning, purpose, self-actualization and transcendence and spirit connection, Circle is a powerful time-tested accelerator. The power of self-belief, nourished and cultivated through the regular practice of Circle moves *you* step by step, power by power, toward the realization of your purpose.

In addition to The Circle Way (https://www.thecircleway.net) another important resource tool for Circles is a guidebook of exercises and practices written by Joanna Macy and Molly Young Brown called *Coming Back to Life—Practices to Reconnect Our Lives, Our World,* which contains the combined experiences of 40 years of workshops and retreats conducted all over the world. (See Resources at www.forthegoodofallnow.org.)

People will self-organize but there is a big difference between asking people to organize a committee to build a movement and asking them to meet in Circle to develop their own superpowers to make change happen locally. It is a different organizational tool. And it is a tool of self-empowerment, extraordinarily more effective than being told to perform a function. This is synergy at work—power-*with*.

To get involved, check www.forthegoodofallnow.org to see if there are Shared wisdom circles near you. You may want to connect and possibly even join an existing circle. If you have a core group, all it takes is at least two of you to start, establish a meeting schedule and begin inviting others to join you.

a. **New Shared Wisdom Circles:** Whether you have experience or not in Circle, you can start one and learn from other Circles. Once you have visited The Circle Way's website, you may want to visit an existing Circle. Please check the Circle visitation requirements on our website at www.forthegoodofallnow. org.

Circle is a safe, sacred space. Confidentiality is an absolute commitment. It is important for participants to understand the process and their responsibilities as a participant and visitor. Starting or calling a Circle can be as simple as asking one other person to join with you and repeating this process until you reach 6 to 8 people. Circles can be smaller or larger. You will find the right mix. This is all common sense. You will call on people with whom you are compatible, people you like and want to spend time with. Other members will do the same and pretty soon you are bonding with people who share a common desire to do good For the Good of All, NOW! Follow the guidelines provided online on our website. Circles collaborate because it is in our nature to cooperate.

b. **Existing Circles:** I understand that there are many purposes for gathering in Circle. If you are in an existing Circle and would like to participate and develop shared wisdom for your community, we welcome you. I realize that tinkering with your routines and processes must be carefully considered. We would love to have experienced Circle participation. Please reach out to us via the website.

c. **Taking reasonable precautions:** For those on the fence, attending a local Circle as a guest would provide a solid experiential grounding. Guests are invited to participate in an outer circle. They must abide by the rules of Circle, including honoring confidentiality. Thus, Circle members must be thoughtful in who they invite. I highly suggest setting aside special 'open house' events. However, we know that there will be significant incentives, especially in oppressive regimes, to disrupt the work of Circles. In all cases, we recognize that these are questions and issues that require a coordination of strategies.

The decision to join in any collective effort is multi-faceted and raises a lot of practical and emotional questions. Three interconnected questions about joining a Circle stand out to me: Will I fit in? What is my role? Is this connected to my purpose? In other words: *How do I plug in?*

## 5. Plugging In

The following roles are provided purely as a way to help you plug in. No one in Circle is going to ask you to adopt a role. These roles are provided as a tool to provide some direction—a comfort zone if you will—because most people in any kind of group setting want to understand how they can best contribute. These are tools to help you, not job descriptions.

*Co-Creators:* everyone engaged in Circle is a *Co-Creator*. At times, people will want to understand how they can fit in more productively. The following five roles are not fixed. They are not job descriptions and there is no hierarchy. Circle members may, and in fact will, move from one role to another. These multiple roles are no different than the roles any of us enjoy as a family member. I can be a husband, granddad, uncle, brother and son all at the same time. Likewise, you will probably have some Guardian, Guide, Emissary and Artist in you.

**Guardians:** keep the Circle on track. They create a safe space and maintain the customs and procedures of Circle. In leadership, you are likely to take charge and maintain a steady course. You value and maintain the institutional procedures of the Circle and tend to the health and welfare of the Circle and its participants. Guardians protect the Circle, which may be a particularly challenging role in times of crisis and *chaos*.

**Guides:** provide light along the path. Adventuresome, you are willing to show the way and to lead others. Capable of evaluating options and charting a course. You have an intuitive understanding of strengths and weaknesses of the team. You tend to be a person of quiet confidence. You are reassuring. When lost, Guides bring you home. Guides help the Circle to stay focused and on point. You are full-throated cheerleaders. Optimists to the more cautious Guardians. (This would be my likely choice.)

**Emissaries:** as described in the Shambhala prophecy, the Shambhala warriors have *"great courage- moral and physical."* The term warrior was appropriate in the 1200-year-old prophecy, but the description of the role of the Shambhala warrior is more akin to an emissary today. So, I have taken the liberty to translate the role into 21st century terms. Emissaries train to acquire the wisdom, strength, and compassion necessary for this work in Circle. Part of going *"into the corridors of power where the decisions are made"* may mean interacting with governments, organizations, and political parties, but all these institutions will also be changing radically as part of the macroshift. You could be living in the kind of pure consensual democracy Gandhi envisioned, sooner than you expect as a result of chaos and collapse. The prophecy ties directly to the traits that we recognize in Gandhi: remain calm and loving in thought and deed; reject destructive thinking.

**Artists:** artists are in a special category. Although all these roles overlap, I cannot emphasize enough that roles are *not* pigeonholes.

They are descriptions of ways to plug in. You may find yourself migrating toward different roles at different times. Everyone is likely to adopt any of the three roles at any time. The Artists, in particular, bring to Circle acute sensory powers, adding a dimension that is unique and critical in interpreting the signs of spirit as they manifest in the world and in the Circle. We all have a little of the Artist in us. Listen to the Artists in your Circle and in yourself as they will interpret signs that many of us may miss. As we hold our hearts out in service to others, as we listen, as we lift each other up when we stumble, and as we connect through our tears and our laughter, we transform ourselves.

> *"The best way to find yourself is to lose yourself in the service of others."*
>
> —Mahatma Gandhi

## 6. Shared Wisdom

### Shared Wisdom Checklist

The product or output of Circle is shared wisdom which expresses the Circle's best effort at describing new ways to live harmoniously with each other and the world. This checklist is a good starting point and is intended as a tool to help Circles develop shared wisdom. It, as well as other materials, will be developed and refined through use and feedback.

❑   Is the norm developed by Thick *We's*—people whose fates are intertwined?

❑   Is this action arrived at by fear of scarcity or with a sense of abundance?

❑   Is the impact driven by power-*over* or power-*with*?

❑ Does it nurture nonviolence and peace?

❑ Are individuals empowered to act for the highest common good of the community?

❑ Does the *outcome* result in the highest possible common good/wellbeing?

The expression of shared wisdom is an expression of the Circle. As such, much freedom of expression is accorded to Circle. The more shared wisdom gets posted, the more likely conventions will emerge, and a common usage and formats will evolve.

There is no need to over-complicate shared wisdom. It is the expression of a Circle that proposes a solution to a community challenge and achieves the Good of All. The focus is at the complete discretion of the Circle, but it must clearly be for the common good—the Good of All. We will be accumulating examples of these resources as a container for Shared Wisdom. I take this opportunity to point out again what a great resource **Yes! Magazine** is for finding inspiration.

# SECTION D: *What changes can We expect to experience?*

## 1. Atomized *I's* to Thick *We's*—*"dancing to an invisible piper"*

When I ask an American when he or she first remembered hearing the term 'holistic', the typical answer is about 20 years or so ago. Our language is very much a representation of the culture we live in. Holism is inevitably a power-*with* operating system because it recognizes the importance of the part being the whole, the whole being a part. Our skin doesn't separate us from the universe, it is part of our connection with and to the universe. We are One with everything. As you know, Thick *We's* are strongly bound together by shared fates.

Increasing chaos will thrust humans together in community, bound by shared fates.

The current state of world affairs is a significant opportunity to think about our shared fates as members of the human race. The prevailing Western norm emphasizes individualism—a social process by which we see ourselves as distinct, special, separate, and unique, no longer bound by shared fates resulting in a society of Atomized I's. Though it may appear to many that individualism rules in this era, in reality social media tells us differently. Our culture, and this is a global phenomenon, is obsessed with being seen, recognized, retweeted, and liked. The Atomized I's seek to rebuild the loss of meaningful connection (power-*with*), but more 'likes' and seeking recognition and fame are kinds of power-*over*. They are weak substitutes. The era of the Cult of Individualism will come to an end soon, as we learn the hard lessons of shedding our *"arrogance."* As we find shelter in the company of each other in Circle, the Thick *We's* will determine the trajectory of humanity. Whether it will be a Great Awakening, or a New Dark Age is entirely up to us.

Atomized I's exist in the physical world thinking that they are separate from others and from nature. But, in this respect, scientists are already well ahead of popular culture. In the universe that includes the spirit dimension, often called the cosmos, oneness prevails. Miracles, dreams, premonitions, after-life, and near-death experiences, all are said to occur when the two show up simultaneously in our physical and spiritual worlds—in the cosmos.

> *"Human beings, vegetables, or cosmic dust, we all dance to a mysterious tune, intoned in the distance by an invisible piper."*
> —Albert Einstein

In 1973, Dr. Edgar Mitchell—one of the astronauts on Apollo 14—set about *"Bridging scientific exploration and experiential discovery to better understand a timeless truth — that humanity is deeply interconnected."* He created the Institute of Noetic Sciences to *"explore the interplay between scientific knowledge and inner knowing."* <u>https://noetic.org</u>

Humans' natural state is oneness, but arrogance misleads us into believing that we are a collection of Atomized I's. Getting to 'We' starts with 'Me.' In Circle, we turn the Atomized I's' into the much richer and interesting 'Thick *We's*' that we have always been. Reconnecting to our shared purposes and shared fates is much easier and far more rewarding than we might expect.

> *The alignment of the physical and spiritual that occurs in Circle launches the practitioner to another level of consciousness and empowerment.*

Reclaiming this power-*with* (each other) and applying it from the bottom up is the highest calling we have as citizens of the world. For the Good of All, NOW! will describe how making change can be replicated in ever-widening circles to embrace the world, and why the *arrogance* of the Atomized I's will not survive the chaos of the storms that are brewing as described in the following ancient fable.

## The Oak and The Reed

*"Well, little one,"* said Oak to Reed growing at its foot, *"Why do you not plant your feet deeply in the ground, and raise your head boldly in the air as I do?"*

*"I am happy with my fate,"* said Reed. *"I may not be so grand, but I think I am safer."*

*"Safe!"* sneered Oak. *"Who shall pluck me up by the roots or bow my head to the ground?"*

*"As he said these very words*
*A violent angry storm arose.*
*The tree held strong; the Reed he bent.*
*The wind redoubled and did not relent,*
*Until finally it uprooted the poor Oak*
*Whose head had been in the heavens*
*And roots among the empire of the dead."*

The *arrogance* of the Oak echoes the arrogance of the culture that Mary Oliver describes in "Of the Empire," which thinks *"little if at all about the quality of life for people (other people), for dogs, for rivers. All the world, in our eyes, they will say, was a commodity."*

A culture that treats people like commodities and teaches them that things are more important than the quality of life, results in people who are self-gratifying, socially alienated, resentful, passive, and powerless.

Tired of feeling in pain, they find the scapegoats, the others, upon whom they will lay the blame for their unhappiness. Very rarely do the people who turn the world into a commodity get blamed for the sickness they have profited handsomely from. If there is blame it is always directed at the weakest, the most vulnerable, those with different skin pigments, the newcomers, the immigrant, the poor. This is the nature of power-*over* which leads to an arrogance that makes them feel mighty and safe, like the oak. But as Aesop's reeds tell the fallen oak: *'You fight and contend with the wind, and consequently you are destroyed; while we on the contrary bend before the least breath of air, and therefore remain unbroken, and escape.'* (Much of this version of the fable is from De la Fontaine's later translation of Aesop's fable.)

In the book *How the Mighty Fall,* the business guru Jim Collins hits the nail on the head: "Every institution is vulnerable to decline, no matter how great. We found that great companies often fall in five stages: 1)

Hubris Born of Success, 2) Undisciplined Pursuit of More, 3) Denial of Risk and Peril, 4) Grasping for Salvation, and 5) Capitulation to Irrelevance or Death." The same can be said of religion, capitalism, nationalism, and globalization. These doctrines will be brought down by self-arrogance, greed, growth and recklessness, self-deception and, ultimately, they will come to signify very little. As one falls, so will the others, as they are all propped up by power-*over* institutions which are by design, rigid and hierarchical. As humanity transitions to *holos*—oneness—which is power-*with*, it will replace the culture that created hearts that were *"small, and hard, and full of meanness,"* giving way to flexibility, nimbleness, vitality and resilience.

The most valuable cultures to inform our survival will likely be the cultures that still have a connection to the *mythos* era, the Indigenous cultures. Their lead in the shift to oneness is important, and it must be heard. (See Resources for the 18 indigenous principles mentioned in Chapter 1 at www.forthegoodofallnow.org.) There is no reason to let anyone, least of all those who wish to exert power-*over*, tell us what our values should be. Let us make clear that scapegoating and blaming each other is no longer productive. As Gandhi remarked: *"An eye for an eye will make the whole world blind."* We are all in this together. The chaos is facing all of us, fighting the battles of yesterday is useless. Clearly, there will be a considerable amount of pain and grievance in the populations seeking to stop or reverse time. But the path of love and compassion will bring us together as one. Compassion is essential if we are to survive. There is no better practice for finding deep compassion than Circle. None of us can change the past, but we can change the future. Most importantly, we can change ourselves. And the easiest way to do this is through the superpower of Circle.

## 2. Surrender:

The genetic predisposition to compete with each other, either within our group or with other groups, developed to ensure the survival of the fittest and is inseparable from human development. At its worst, competition exhorts us to violence. At its best, it exhorts us to be and do better. This concept can be found in the Eastern martial arts like Judo, meaning the *Way of Gentleness*, where the focus is on balance and disarming your opponent by giving in to the power being exerted against you, and leveraging it to throw the attacker off balance—power-*with*. Judo is not a weakness. Surrender is not a weakness. Balance is not a weakness. They are evidence of a different power source—balance—which is achieved only by power-*with*.

*If humanity survives it will be because enough of us surrender to, rather than struggle against the flow.*

*Surrender* also means knowing your place. For the elders, like me, it is time to pass the torch to younger generations. They will be the implementers of the change we need to see. I cannot do what needs to be done to organize and galvanize a local-to-global movement. I can write this book and publish it. I can offer to support it in every way I can. I can work with others, and I can do my part in my community. I can offer an easily understood universal goal and describe the simple strategy expressed in For the Good of All, NOW!, but if it succeeds it will be because of the engagement and collaboration of others as participants and leaders.

## 3. Community Reputation

*The Fourth Turning* provides a thorough playbook for understanding the Great Turning. In this time of great chaos Strauss and Howe are very clear that <u>your community reputation is by far the most precious asset to have.</u>

During a paradigm shift, especially in this macroshift, understanding the past provides a strong basis for understanding how to navigate the future. The effects of the pandemic, death, fear, anger, adjusting and adapting to new customs and practices, violent weather, all-consuming fires, drought, soil erosion, sea level rise, the mass migration of billions of people, and the expansion of war, mixed in with the cynical intentional attempt of the forces of power-*over* to drive the wedge of antisocial grievance in an effort to preserve their privilege, all point to the need to be very strategic. For the Good of All, NOW! is a call to action to come together as people, organizations and communities to co-create a critical mass that begins moving together from smallest part to the whole, because when the part changes, the whole changes. Once again, the center of human connection and power-*with* will be community.

### *The path to a life well-lived goes through uplifting the common good.*

Expect the dominoes to continue falling quickly as the impacts of the invasion of Ukraine establish the sudden break with the past predicted in the *Resolution*. Widespread societal stress will be felt everywhere by everyone. Social systems will be failing as their resources and capabilities diminish. Circle will become your haven, your refuge, your source of power. Family and community are the others. Share your new skills. Teach others. Get to know all the other wisdom circles and trust in your community. Your spiritual, mental and physical flexibility to bounce back—your resilience—is important. Circle will be your source for restoration. In times of great stress, humans—but not all humans—tend to rise to the occasion. Be a resource for others—this is so important, and it will establish your community reputation. The key is to develop positive relationships with as many people as you can. Circle enables each of us to become maestros, conductors, counselors, like the wise rabbi. As a caretaker you act in fairness amid the *chaos* helping others focus on what they can do, rather than what they are losing. As a member of Circle, sharing your wisdom For the Good of All, NOW! you will establish a strong community reputation. Your work in Circle strengthens your superpowers of interconnection and you co-create incredible synergy.

> *"Synergy is what happens when one plus one equals ten or a hundred or even a thousand! It's the profound result when two or more respectful human beings determine to go beyond their preconceived ideas to meet a great challenge."*
> —Stephen R. Covey

As you read this book, you already have knowledge that most don't have. Please use it wisely and generously. It is not new wisdom. It is a vision as simple and universal as the prayer of Saint Francis of Assisi—*"Lord make us the instruments of your peace. Where there is hatred, let us sow love..."*—or the Golden Rule, which appears in some version in every culture: *to treat others as you would want to be treated.* It is the story of *Our Lady of Unity and Peace.* In it there is hope and there is power-*with.* The mahatmas—Gandhi and Martin Luther King Jr.—are holding the vision and the love force for you, to guide humanity through to a nonviolent, peaceful world, where power is vested in the individual and wielded to do good For the Good of All, NOW!

> *To be fully human in this transition time is to enter into practices that reconnect us to our natural state and to our world.*

## 4. The Rise of Egalitarianism

The stark reality that our 'leaders' are incapable of leading us through this transition is one of the most important revelations of this era, but it is an old story retold in many cultures through the ages as *The Emperor Has No Clothes.* In Western culture, Hans Christian Anderson in *Fairy Tales Told For Children* (1837) made this story famous, but it is much older having been covered by the Roman fable writer, Aesop and in older Indian and Arabic folklore. The Emperor's costume weavers fool him into parading naked by convincing him that his clothes have supernatural powers making them invisible only to the ignorant masses. He is all too willing to go along with his weavers because he doesn't want to admit to being one of the ignorants and nor do his underlings. As the parade winds through the city, a little boy cries out *"the emperor has no clothes."* The fantasy is dispelled, and the emperor is seen for the fool he is. This is similar to many revelations like the Wizard of Oz who appears a rather unassuming old man, quite unlike what he projects to the world from behind his curtain. And, I would argue, like the insights about the nature of power-*over* and power-*with*, of right relationship, fairness, compassion and the importance of Thick *We*'s.

Societies built on power-*with*—an egalitarian system—are not new, they have existed throughout history, built on the premise that life, survival, and extinction are all intertwined, entangled, with nature. These societies have existed in the past and can be found today in the management of all kinds of commons as was proven in the Nobel-winning work of Elinor Ostrom. This history has been buried in the noise of tens of thousands of years of hierarchy which enabled the thinking that humans were incapable of treating each other fairly and equally. For as smart and all-powerful as humanity thinks it is today, it is more like the oak than the reed. Rigidly bound by a self-infatuation with hierarchy and its sense of superiority, the coming-of-age period of *theos* and *logos*, is about to give way to the maturity of *holos*, which recognizes the fullness of all nature's relationships. We are capable of both strength and flexibility. In other words, power-*over* will no longer reign supreme and all the scaffolding it built to support its top-heavy structure will collapse, exposing what has always been true: We are One.

## 5. Self-Rule & The Power of Community

For the Good of All, NOW! is not a magic pill to cure all wrongs, but it is, in conjunction with a more prosocial world, a simple strategy that will lead to a different new world order. It presents a local-to-global movement where thousands of organizations toiling to do good for the Good of All collaborate as a single superorganism. Unless we reinvent a new Gandhi for this time, we are left to begin weaving this tapestry together. I can't imagine a more plausible designer for the future local-to-global order than Gandhi. If it gains traction, it will be forcefully rebutted by those who have the most to lose. Its most powerful argument will be to claim that power-*over* (hierarchy) has produced the greatest growth the world has ever experienced, lifting billions out of $1 a day poverty, neglecting to mention that the poor are still poor at $3 a day. They will claim that it was accomplished by using power-*with* (holarchy). But this is a false argument. It is like cancer asking us to be a host because our cells are super-efficient at spreading its deadly purpose. Our holistic bodies are super-efficient, but cancer is not healthy, it exerts power-*over* to serve its purposes of all-consuming growth. Recognize the difference between power-*over* and power-*with* by its means, purposes and outcomes. If the outcome is defined at the top level of the hierarchy, it can only be achieved through power-*over*. If the outcome is defined and implemented from the lowest level, it will take root and grow strong especially if it is For the Good of All. It is achieved through power-*with*. It is impossible to do good for the Good of All if the outcome and purpose are to do good for the Good of the Few. Remember Gandhi's three legged stool: nonviolence, vest power in the individual, do good for the good of all.

It is fair to say that there is more at work in our universe than we can explain, it is the role of science to help us discover how it works. It is simply *"arrogance"* that makes us claim that only things that can be observed and calculated by us are real. The world was flat before it was round! The unobservable—the unseen—exists and humans find ways to explain it, calling it *karma*, fate, spirit, the same unexplainable spirit Einstein and

Schrödinger wrote about, the same spirit that has dwelled in humans and nature since the beginning of creation. It is the same spirit that animates the practice of Circle, creating the same synergy it always has. When the 'butterfly wings flap' and humans align with Spirit, almost anything can happen. That I can paint a rational picture of what we might expect in the near future is hardly remarkable. But I am far from alone in claiming that there is a power beyond our science that can play a role. Eastern cultures have preserved that connection far better than the Eurocentric cultures, this is why For the Good of All, NOW! draws so liberally on their philosophies and wisdom. It is no coincidence that such wisdom exists, even if it is not widely adopted in the West. It is why, ultimately, I believe humanity will emerge as a fully interconnected, interrelated, natural superorganism living in harmony naturally. This prediction is hardly new, it simply reconnects modern human with roots that go back a million years.

Yet, even as the world experiences chaos and we hear about exceeding climate thresholds that occurred tens of thousands of years ago, we seek refuge in retreat. This is precisely the wrong strategy. The increased suffering, we are experiencing will only end when we accept it and embrace it, while also understanding that we are all interconnected, part of a oneness most of us have rarely if ever experienced. The objective surely has to start with engaging in practices that move us toward True or Deep Community. There are billions of people doing this now. The challenge of coming to terms with our personal, communal, and societal roles will come into clear focus as the chaos grows.

# Section E: What are you For?

## 1. Reimagining the Future Takes A Little Courage

There are, I think, two main obstructions to buying into the idea that the world is about to change quite radically and then actually choosing to engage: arrogance and fear.

**Fear:** The first obstruction to engagement is an echo of the monks—'*O God, not me*'—namely, the *fear* that comes from a lack of self-belief. Forget what others think, this is a time for thinking for yourself. Our culture has a huge impact on our personal level of self-belief. It is one of the great ironies of the era of the cult of individualism is that it leads us not to greater independence, but to a greater need for acceptance as measured by how many 'likes' or retweets we can collect. The more we are separated from our interrelationships and interconnections with each other, the more our levels of self-belief are shattered. Technology has brought us superficially closer while disconnecting us from meaningful contact and entrapping us in a constant cycle of seeking recognition from others now rather than focusing on what will make us happier and more serene in the long term. I suggest that there is no better, easier, more directly applicable self-empowerment game plan to uplift and empower human beings to be the best they can be, than the practice of Circle.

**Arrogance:** The second obstacle is to overcome the arrogance that confuses our personal worldview with our perception of reality. We come to every situation with a set of preconceived notions that allow us to interpret the world around us. My preconceptions as a white European living in an advanced economy will be very different from the preconceptions of a Hindu woman who grew up in the slums of Kolkata. Thus, though I cannot speak for any other culture, I can relate to the commonly held worldviews of my Western culture. No matter your race, your location, your culture, I encourage every reader to make their own assessment of where they stand stripped of as many preconceptions as possible.

Most Westerners are likely to have a steady consistent worldview that tomorrow will be pretty much like today and almost invariably better. There is, in this preconception, a good dose of self-deception and optimism. Anyone can experience a life-shattering event in the next few hours, but the odds are not likely, and it would be foolish to live this way. So, we make rational assumptions that our world will be much the same tomorrow as today and this carries over into our longer-term perception of life, including imagining a better future for ourselves and our children. The reality is often different. The millennial generation growing up today is all too aware that they are not likely to do better than their parents. Yet, we discount to a very large degree even routine reversals of fortune and the consequences of any possible distasteful fate. If something bad is going to happen, it will happen elsewhere, to other people. This bias for self-deceit does not serve us well in chaotic times. It is akin to staying in the path of the storm or the wildfire, certain that we will survive its consequences. Is this not simply a form of arrogance? The arrogance Kabir warned us about so many centuries ago:

"Let your arrogance go, and look around inside...
Those who hope to be reasonable about it fail.
The arrogance of reason has separated us from that love.
With the word "reason" you already feel miles away..."

I strongly suggest to those who think we are just going through a rough patch, to revisit how their assumptions may be leading them astray. To ignore the cycles of history, the unprecedented threat of human-induced climate change, the tendency of complex systems to be affected by tiny fluctuations is foolish. The fundamentalist who clings to an irrational past is engaging in self-deception. No amount of truth and evidence is enough to break this spell. The ranks of these fundamentalists may grow led by the elites who seek only to preserve their power-*over*. However, part of the magnificence of human beings is the heightened ability to perceive different scenarios, to learn from the past, to speculate about future consequences and events. I suggest that NOW might be a good time to take a serious assessment of the situation and decide whether you think the potential rosy scenarios, such as a sudden giant leap in technology among others, will save us from ourselves. If you are in the camp that believes we will soon return to normal, all you have to do is fasten your seatbelt and hope for a soft landing. If you are worried about what is in store, then there are only two options: (1) an urgent need to prepare on a scale to match the unprecedented combination of factors we are facing now; (2) a clear-headed understanding of our current circumstances, how we got here, and an explicit and transparent plan for the future that truly results in the common good. Dame Conrad's "*Being For*" is a good starting point for your consideration.

It does not take much imagination to understand that the current chaos is going to have repercussions. I have provided many examples of the risks we are facing and many of the most obvious changes we could adopt to set a new course, individually and collectively. What I can't do is change the oaks into reeds. The oaks will stubbornly resist until it is too late. The reeds, who far outnumber the oaks, can and must start preparing for the transition in much greater numbers and to greater effect. The oaks are too arrogant to give up their power-*over*, but the reeds have the greater numbers and the greater resilience to survive using their power-*with* each other and the world. The only ones who can save humanity are humans. So, I challenge you to imagine that you are a reed, collaborating *with* the other reeds. Imagine for example, what might happen if *your* community started to measure happiness and wellbeing with a goal of co-creating the common good? The economic growth of a community is meaningless if it is not tied to the common good. It is especially meaningless if the benefits of growth are unequally shared. In the pandemic, we began to reacquaint ourselves with the importance of essential workers. It turns out bankers and politicians are not critical— the teachers, nurses, doctors, bus drivers, maintenance workers, grocery store workers—on the other hand are. Really, it is this simple: Do you want to live in a community that is forever seeking the Good of the Few or do you want to live in a community that is forever seeking to do good For the Good of All?

Fear cannot be overcome with more fear, but there will be plenty of fear spread by the antisocial elements seeking power-*over*. The logical path forward is not more antisocial behavior, but the adoption of prosocial behavior, meaning that we re-learn how to live together with more balance and harmony. Prosocial comes from power-*with*. Communities connecting and coordinating for the common good are more likely to achieve significant change, faster and more peacefully!

Those who only know power-*over* have to impose from the top down. They do not understand power-*with*. As they can't comprehend it, they are left defenseless and their distractions will ultimately fail.

> *"Remember that all through history, there have been tyrants and murderers, and for a time, they seem invincible. But in the end, they always fall. Always."*
>
> —Gandhi

What are *You* For?

# CHAPTER 3

# DEEP CONNECTION

*"You may say I'm a dreamer*
*But I'm not the only one*
*I hope someday you'll join us*
*And the world will live as one."*

Imagine—written by Yoko Ono and John Lennon;
produced by Phil Spector, 1971

## Section A: *Who* are *We*?

### 1. The Great Turning

*"Future generations, if there is a livable world for them, will look back at the epochal transition we are making to a life-sustaining society. And they may well call this the time of the Great Turning."*— Joanna Macy https://www.joannamacy.net/

*"Our time has come to trade the sorrows of Empire for the joys of Earth Community. Let our descendants look back on this time as the time of the Great Turning, when humanity made a bold choice to*

*birth a new era devoted to actualizing the higher potentials of our human nature.*

*The work begins with embracing the truth that it is within our means to choose our future and to place our capacity for reflective choice at the service of Creation's continued unfolding. We are the ones we have been waiting for."*

*The Great Turning—From Empire to Earth Community,* David C. Korten (See Resources: www.forthegoodofallnow.org.)


## 2. The Great Devaluation

The repetitive cycles of boom-and-bust that always end up with a bail-out of the capitalists who caused them, most recently the Great Depression (1929) and the Great Recession (2008-2009) to name but the two most obvious global busts, are about to be eclipsed by the size of the **Great Devaluation**, as Strauss and Howe referred to this coming event.

What Strauss and Howe called the millennial saeculum and I refer to as the *Pax Americana*, a term for the absence of a World War that was ensured in large part by America's military might and its contributions and support of globalization. There is another factor that rivals America's and Europe's domination during this period and that is its currency—the U.S. dollar, which became the currency of globalization. The U.S. and Europe established and currently run the International Monetary Fund and the World Bank. In the last decade or so, the U.S. dollar, while still the reigning global currency, has seen its exclusive authority in global economic monetary transactions eroded—for example, Russia and China are now using the Chinese Yuan in commodities trading, especially oil. Meanwhile, the rise of inflation, recession, and deglobalization will precipitate economic, political and social disruptions that are frankly difficult to imagine.

## 3. Growth-Greed-Capitalism

It used to be that currencies were tied to a country's gold reserves as a guarantee that the bank notes could redeemed for something of real value. Since 1971, the U.S. dollar has been backed by the good faith and trust of the government. Essentially, today the Federal Reserve creates more dollars by just making an entry on a register at the Central Bank and distributing new bills through the banking system. This is like what the German government did after WWI: it started printing money with abandon. The result was that you needed a wheelbarrow of banknotes to buy a loaf of bread. Why and how currencies collapse is complicated, but it happens regularly and pumping the economy with additional currency is one sure fire way to devalue it. Recent reports (see Wall Street Parade articles, Reddit, etc.) have calculated that the Federal Reserve has created 22% of all dollars issued since 1776 in 2020 alone! In the 2007-2009 crisis $29 trillion were printed to bail out the risky bets of the financiers on Wall Street. Since 2019, another mere (!) $9 trillion have been printed to cover the pandemic. Even if you have no idea about how the Federal Reserve works, magically creating new money with the stroke of a pen and pumping it into the economy must be shocking to the average person. The **Growth-Greed-Capitalism** scheme, as I have come to describe the house of cards that characterizes the U.S. economy and the political system that supports it, will not survive the shock of war *and* the cascading costs of dealing with climate change, *and* currency manipulation, *and* the systemic attacks by conservatives and the Rupert Murdoch media empire on the institutions of democracy, because they seek by any means to conserve wealth and power for themselves.

There is no reason to expect that governments and the elites are prepared to level with the people about the impending disasters and the changes necessary to avoid them. It is not in their best interests to do so, and they have deep vested interests in believing that the current paradigm will go on forever. Reality is about to crash headlong into the intoxicating effects of self-importance and the use of power-*over*. This is quite likely during the midterm U.S. elections in 2022 and will most certainly affect the 2024 election cycle. Whether it is vanity, thrill-seeking, overconfidence in the capacity of technology to solve any problem (the Myth of Icarus), the embrace of greed as a positive value, or all of the above, the reality is there is no Planet B and the weaknesses of all our institutions limit their ability to change with the times.

## The Goose and the Golden Egg

*There was once a farmer who had a wonderful goose that laid a golden egg every day. And every day the farmer would sell the egg in the market. He soon became rich. The richer he got the greedier he got. Believing he could get all the gold at once; he killed the goose and opened it to find nothing.*

Self-importance, or hubris—excessive *pride*—added to the farmer's *greed,* with a sprinkling of *gluttony, lust, envy, laziness* thrown in, all urging the farmer to act in a self-destructive way. This is the same hubris—vanity and conceitedness—of the small group of self-anointed 'leaders of the world' representing the one-percenters (who hold 43% of the world's wealth), who continue to huddle in Davos Switzerland (or on Zoom) to feed the fantasy that the thinking that brought humanity to the threshold of extinction is about to lead the world into a glorious elite-inspired 'Stakeholder Capitalism' and a 'Fourth Industrial Revolution' (both topics are easily accessible online). The great irony is that this is the same group (The Club of Rome) that commissioned Donella Meadows et al to produce and publish *"Limits to Growth"* (1972, '74,' 92, '04, '05), which forecasted *"global societal collapse by the mid twentieth century."* The latest update by Gaya Herington (the Director of Advisory, Sustainability Services at KPMG, a business services provider), published in *The Journal of Industrial Ecology* (2021), indicates *"a halt in growth over the next decade or so, which puts into question the usability of continuous growth as humanity's goal in the 21st century."*

Furthermore, the scenario she tested that included pollution induced climate change *"depicts a collapse scenario."* A sliver of the optimistic scenario *"suggests that it's almost, but not yet too late for society to change course."* The end of growth is the end of modern-day capitalism upon which it rests and by extension the end of globalization. (See Resources for links to Donella Meadows work.)

**Greed** is 'freeloading' on a grand scale. It results in the "Tragedy of the Commons" and contradicts the second core design principle of an equal, or fair, distribution of the benefits and costs associated from an activity. Elinor Ostrum proved that the "Tragedy of the Commons," which asserted that humans were too flawed to successfully manage their commons, was wrong. When the ignorant and bad faith farmer kills the goose, he destroys the source of his own wealth. The goose was his commons. When the goose or the commons are butchered, freeloading ends, because there is nothing left to distribute to anyone including to the freeloaders! In the world we live in today, 47% of the world's wealth is controlled by millionaires. According to the Federal Reserve Bank of St Louis, in 2016 the top 10% of Americans owned 77% of the wealth, the next 40% owned 22% of wealth, the bottom 50% owned 1% and 1 in 10 of those families had negative net worth. (Do you really need to ask where all that 'free money' the Fed keeps pumping out ends up?) Inequality on this scale has never ended well for the wealthy, but financial crises always hurt the poor the most. The biggest red flag for even a casual observer should be the constant cycle of financial failures that occur regularly and frequently. The coming crash, or series of crashes over the next few years, will result, as it did in Germany in the 1920s, in devaluing national currencies across the globe. This makes a compelling case for alternative local currencies, like Berkshares and others. (See Resources www. forthegoodofallnow.org.) The popularity of cyber currencies may provide a basis for an alternative global trade exchange mechanism, but currently they incur huge computer operating costs, and their values are wildly volatile. It seems to me their strongest claim, as currently structured, is more as a high stakes speculative investment vehicle perfectly matched to the Greed-Growth-Capitalism ideology. The benefit of these decentralized cyber currencies may, like everything else in society, be repurposed for the Good of All.

**Growth:** Wishing for constant growth is like wishing for cancer. It makes no sense! Except to the capitalists who accumulate vast fortunes from it. The more rational objective is to grow the common good—the wellbeing of all. This is what a healthy society and a healthy ecosystem need!

**Capitalism:** Adam Smith (*The Wealth of Nations* 1776), wrote that humans were endowed with "an iron fist" of morality that would temper their pursuit of wealth. Today, the notion seems quaint, were it not for it being so dreadful in terms of its consequences in the free-for-all theft of wealth by the *elites*.

### Growth-Greed-Capitalism is killing the world it depends on.

This statement will be met with the howls of those who stand to lose the most—the power-*over* classes in politics, business, and the elites. They will scream *communism* and *socialism* don't work, which misses the point entirely. The replacement of this power-*over* system with another power-*over* system, which both communism and socialism became, is clearly not a solution. It is the power-*with* of localism and self-rule in pursuit of the wellbeing of all—humans and nature—that will re-establish balance. The more we learn about nature, the clearer it becomes that we should put in place the same efficiencies—power-*with* and holarchy, instead of power-*over* and hierarchy. Competition and comparison can be tools or weapons. When used to exert power-*over*, they become weapons of division and disharmony. However, when we choose to use competition and comparison to exert power-*with*, they create balance and become tools of unity and harmony. Unity and peace are within reach if humans choose to make it so. As we are natural beings, it makes sense that we should live by nature's design principles, including vesting power-*with* at the lowest levels. In fact, the arrogance of believing we are separate from the laws of nature, is precisely why humanity finds itself at this critical juncture. Reconnecting to each other and to nature in the realization that we are one and always have been interconnected and interdependent is the only path forward. The curtain is being pulled back, the smoke and mirrors that created the illusion that we are separate is now seen for what it has always been, a way to subjugate, conquer, enslave, suppress, exploit. The new day is dawning when liberation will reconnect us to our natural selves, to each other and to the world through Circle.

> *The refuge of Circle is the personal safe harbor, and prosocial self-rule the only form of governance, that will sustain communities through the Great Turning into holos.*

## 4. Nationalism and Politics

The end of the *Revolutionary* saeculum—1704 to 1794—was a particularly *chaotic* and exciting time, *"the best of times and the worst of times."* This era set up the foundations of Eurocentrism. The art of politics is of course much older, but it is in this era, when the reins of governance that had been established during *theos* as a partnership between state and religion, sought to throw off the shackles of feudalism and diminish the role of religion in civic affairs. The differences in the schools of thought about how to govern society underwent a vibrant 250 years of experimentation and evolution. Fundamental religious states continued with their feet firmly planted in the past. The modern state—nationalism—emerged as either a continuation of the *theos* inspired autocrat as a supreme leader (fundamentalism), or the more *logos* inspired non-religious autocracies and democracies with elected presidents and representatives of the people (European style democracy). While the differences are important, it must be recognized that the tools of democracy were, and continue to be, subverted and influenced by all sorts of organizations and groups seeking to gain more power-*over*. What we call democracy, which arose in ancient Greece (507 BCE), was preceded by both top-down run governance—emperors and tyrants—and egalitarian societies where social equality and rights reigned. In *The Dawn of Everything*, by David Graeber and David Wengrow, the authors offer *"proof that a highly egalitarian society has been possible on an urban scale"* across the world. Such societies like the city of Ur which lasted from 2025 to 1738 BCE, in Ancient Sumeria (modern-day Iraq) was one of these zones. In fact, for most of humanity's existence egalitarian societies have been the norm and were characteristic of both our hunter-gatherer and foraging ancestors. Some aspects of these cultures still remain like the Kalahari, Aborigine, and the Native Indigenous tribes of the Americas. This is great news to those who assume that humans have to be controlled by other human beings. The *holos* macroshift will effectively renew humanity's egalitarian instincts by using power-*with* as developed in small groups—Circles—in communities that can then manage their own affairs (their commons) using the Eight Core Design Principles. When Gandhi proposed self-rule, he would not have been aware of the Eight Core Design Principles, but he knew it was possible for people to achieve self-rule based on three principles: Coexist nonviolently and peacefully. Vest power in the individual. Seek the highest common good. These old and new technologies should and will improve on the egalitarian impulses of our ancestors.

**When self-rule meets the eight Core Design Principles, the two technologies combine to make nations and politics unnecessary.**

That we can use wisdom from 1730 BCE to replace the wisdom of the 1730 CE era (the Age of Enlightenment) that gave rise to nationalism and capitalism adds an irresistible balance and rhythm to the cycles of time. But it goes deeper than that, because the rhythms of evolution are also unseating the recent fascination with hierarchical design, which is roughly 10,000 years old, while restoring the holistic design features—interconnection, interdependence, oneness—that have been with us for over a million years.

## 5. Ecological Design

Jeremy Lent, author and integrator, poses a question that is fully congruent with For the Good of All, NOW!—"Our mainstream worldview has expired. What will replace it?" In *The Web of Meaning, Integrating Science and Traditional Wisdom to Find Our Place in the Universe,* (https://www.jeremylent.com ), Jeremy answers five essential questions: *"Who Am I? Where Am I? How Should I Live? Why Am I? Where Are We Going?"* These remind us of the questions the great artist Paul Gauguin (1848-1903) inscribed on his famous Tahitian Tableau and E.O. Wilson used to frame his fundamental contribution to the understanding of human evolution in *The Social Conquest of Earth*—Where Do We Come From? What Are We? Where Are We Going? Frankly, *The Web of Meaning* is like having a handbook to use alongside Prosocial and ACT (Acceptance and Commitment Therapy) training for all who wish to help build societies that do good For the Good of All, NOW! (See Resources at www.forthegoodofallnow.org.)

In the article "What an Ecological Civilization Looks Like", in the Spring 2021 YES! Magazine, Mr. Lent described the six rules that will become important touchstones for Circles to use to develop shared wisdom, which I have abbreviated here.

### *Six Rules for Rejoining the Natural World—Jeremy Lent*

i.  **Diversity**: *"A system's health depends on differentiation and integration."*

ii.  **Balance:** *"Every part of a system is in a harmonious relationship with the entire system."*

iii. **Fractal Organization:** *"The small reflects the large, and the health of the whole system requires the flourishing of each part."*

iv.  **Life Cycles:** *"Regenerative and sustainable flourishing into the long-term future."*

v.   **Subsidiarity:** *"Issues at the lowest level affect health at the top."*

vi.  **Symbiosis**: *"Relationships that work for mutual benefit."*

# Section B: *Where are We going?*

## THE SPOONS

A holy man was having a conversation with his Lord one day and said, "Lord, I would like to know what Heaven and Hell are like."

The Lord led the holy man to two doors. He opened one of the doors and the holy man looked in. In the middle of the room was a large round table. In the middle of the table was a large pot of stew which smelled delicious and made the holy man's mouth water.

The people sitting around the table were thin and sickly. They appeared to be famished. They were holding spoons with very long handles that were strapped to their arms and each found it possible to reach into the pot of stew and take a spoonful, but because the handle was longer than their arms, they could not get the spoons back into their mouths.

The holy man shuddered at the sight of their misery and suffering. The Lord said, "You have seen Hell."

They went to the next room and opened the door. It was exactly the same as the first one. There was the large round table with the large pot of stew which made the holy man's mouth water. The people were equipped with the same long-handled spoons, but here the people were well nourished and plump, laughing and talking. The holy man said, "I don't understand."

"It is simple," said the Lord. "It requires but one skill. You see, they have learned to feed each other. While the greedy think only of themselves."

**It is normal for every paradigm shift to be as a blind spot in the mirror, invisible to the driver.**

## 1. The Wheel of Human Relationship

At the center of the Circle of Life are the three relationships that bind all humanity with the Universe: shared fates, spirit, and right relationship. It takes trust and humility to believe that the essence of a good life is a function of these relationships. The Wheel of Human Relationship is as simple as the lesson of The Spoons and just as powerful—both show the impact of power-*with*. It re-awakens the true nature of our essence as part of nature and thus deeply interconnected, interdependent, interrelated to everything, physical and spiritual. And it assigns us a simple important role: caretaker.

In Chapter 1, right relationship is described as: "A thing is right when it tends to preserve the integrity, resilience, and beauty of the commonwealth of life. It is wrong when it tends otherwise." Understanding right relationship is the key to a life well-lived. Right relationship involves both the physical and spiritual dimensions of our lives; the interconnectedness and interdependence of all life; our essential interbeing, as Thich Nhat Hahn described it. The physical and spiritual aspects are interconnected in one body. The relationship of a human being to life is, like a permanent metaphorical umbilical cord, always interconnected to all of nature as a part of the cosmos and in a union of the physical and the metaphysical. Einstein made this clear: "The laws of nature manifest the existence of a spirit vastly superior to that of men."

The Five Interrelationships described below all flow from the oneness of spirit, shared fates and right relationship and represent what I call the Wheel of Human Relationship. The interconnectedness of the physical and spiritual dimensions is the guiding light on the path to harmony and serenity, happiness and peace.

*Harmony and serenity, happiness and peace are accessed through practice. There are no shortcuts.*

The caretaker exists at the intersection of power-*over* and power-*with*. There is a responsibility to watch over, to guide, to care for and nurture not unlike the role of a parent. Doesn't this make much more sense as a model for our interrelationships with each other and all life on Earth? Gandhi reimagined the commercial enterprise as evolving into a trusteeship. In other words, rather than the owners managing the enterprise's assets for the benefit of the owners, the trustees of a business would manage its assets for the common good of the employees and all stakeholders, including society and nature. The trustees are in effect, caretakers. Hierarchical management is essential in a power-*over* system, but it is incompatible with and contrary to a power-*with* system, a holarchy. Just like self-rule is achieved by vesting the power of self-governance at the lowest levels, so will the organizations of the future vest power at the lowest level. And this will be because there is no more efficient design for organized group activity.

This is great news for humanity! When we realize our essential role as caretaker for each other and for the world, we are preserving "...the integrity, resilience, and beauty of the commonwealth of life." When we gather in Circle, we affirm and refine this right relationship to each other, our planet, our cosmos.

# THE FIVE STAGES OF HUMANITY'S RIGHT RELATIONSHIP TO LIFE

**Cradled:** Infancy. From conception to birth, we exist in the right-relationship of oneness to all of creation on the physical and spiritual planes. Coming to life in the world happens as the heart 'magically' closes a trapdoor between the right and the left sides of the heart, which sends a signal to the lungs to suck in air as the body recognizes that oxygen will no longer be delivered through the umbilical cord. Our initial interrelationship was to nature and spirit, our second interrelationship was to our birth parents—who are our first caretakers. As we do not know what spirit intends, losing a child is a deep loss. It is best to have engaged in good practices and right-relationships with loving, compassionate caretakers in these moments when love, compassion, and awareness of interrelationships physically and spiritually are essential.

**Carried:** Childhood. At the beginning we are literally carried, but we soon find our feet and begin exploring. We are helpless and thus would have great difficulty surviving or preparing, without some help, for the responsibilities that will be coming our way. This is the beginning of our personal path. During this time there is much experimentation—this is nature's way to teach us. We have the liberty in our family and expanding clan, to test what works and what doesn't. We begin to define our future roles through a period, often chaotic, of experimentation. We would likely perish were it not for the powerful bonds of healthy right relationships.

**Co-creators:** Young Adults. We have developed the independence to begin taking care of ourselves and offspring. We are ready to assume one of our most important evolutionary roles, procreation, to ensure the continuation of our species. As young adults and procreators we rely on the bonds of healthy relationships to raise our young with the help of our clan. It is wise to have good caretakers around to help bring our babies into the world and to share in their development.

**Caretakers:** Adults. Creating the right relationships with other human beings and nature in support of life is the main shared responsibility of caretakers. If we have offspring, we are responsible for nurturing and raising them. Our interrelationship with our family, clan, tribe, and the community of life is vital in the nurturing of the offspring. *It takes a village to raise a child*, is not just an old proverb or the title of a book, it recognizes the deeply rooted shared wisdom of human beings as caretakers who *must* rely on the bonds of healthy interrelationships in order to care for our species. Right relationships were central to Gandhi's teaching. It is a shared human responsibility to help co-create a world where *all* can thrive. Our right relationship to creation, from the atoms to the cosmos, is as caretaker. As we had no hand in creating the universe we live in, so *we have no individual ownership of any part of the universe*, but we are caretakers of it for future generations. We may have a temporary lease to use and nurture nature, but as caretakers our responsibility is to help nature thrive For the Good of All. Indigenous peoples have passed down this ancient knowledge and can help us rekindle it.

**Cradled:** Old Age. There comes a time when life ends. The passage back to our spirit form occurs in many ways, sometimes suddenly and violently, but typically it is preceded by the aging process. (I note here that one of the great revelations in my life was when I realized that spirit dictates why we are, where we are, and what happens to us.) As we prepare for this eventuality, we realize that we will need to be cradled once again. Indeed, we are lucky to have loved ones present, just as we did at our birth, supporting and helping us return to spirit. Elders still have a vital role to play. We—because I am an elder—are no longer responsible directly for the welfare of the children, but we have voices. We have knowledge. Hopefully by now we have gathered some wisdom which we can share as other caretakers assist us in rejoining spirit.

As we are not perfect beings, it is important to be able to distinguish between what harms and what builds right relationships. Being a caretaker is not a complicated concept, it hardly needs explaining. It is a role that lays the foundation for what it means to be a full participant in the new *holos* paradigm. It is broad enough to envelop any of the other suggested roles for Circle participants—guardian, guide, emissary, artist. It establishes the broad nature of the responsibilities for maintaining harmony, balance, peace, unity, not just for this generation but for all generations who will preserve our right relationship with all of life. The path to restoring whatever it is you are 'for' is grounded in the ethic of caretaker-ship for our planet and all life.

In community, *'locals'* have the primary duty of care to maintain the Good of All for their own commons using shared wisdom and self-rule. Every commons exists as part of a complex and diverse system made up of ever-widening circles of commons interconnected in a web of interbeing. This structure is replicated in the movement as elected member representatives from local shared wisdom Circles form a local-to-global hive of ever-widening circles of People's Committees.

Every Circle has instantaneous access to the Shared wisdom of other Circles on the electronic platform of the Web of Interbeing®. When a self-rule community struggles to find the 'right' formula with other Circles, both locally and nonlocally, it is easy enough to use the Eight Core Design

Principles as the technology to move us toward a solution that achieves the common good.

The Ecological Design Principles and the Eighteen Indigenous Principles refine the Shared wisdom of Circles. In addition, the guidance of the Circle's member representatives to the People's Committees is particularly useful as the People's Committees represent a vast pool of wisdom and practice to help guide and connect all caretakers and Circles in the Web of Interbeing®. This "hive" will work to co-create a Wikipedia style platform that will instantaneously post the shared wisdom of all participants creating direct feedback loops. This is vastly different from the kind of process employed in today's power-*over*, hierarchical systems.

Why is this idea of becoming caretakers so simple to state and potentially difficult to adapt to? Because we need to learn these lessons just like a baby learns to walk, a child experiments, a teenager tests the limits, and an adult applies the learning to co-exist with others and raise future generations to do the same. The timeframes for the *Great Turning* demand urgency. But, at its core the basic truths remain:

*The wellbeing of the world is dependent on the wellbeing of people and communities. The path to wellbeing, physically and spiritually, is through right relationship.*

The practice of Circle means that it won't be long before you will be looking at long-held practices and norms through this lens as well as the lens of prosocial. That is when the real fun begins and your Circle becomes a fountain of inspiration For the Good of All, NOW! These personal and societal rewards rely on dedicating time and practice to interact deeply with people. If circumstances dictate not meeting in person, then convene on any of the electronic platforms that provide alternatives— Zoom, Facebook, etc.

As previously mentioned, the world-renowned work of Christina Baldwin's book *Calling the Circle* and http://www.thecircleway.net/ is a good starting place. Dr. Julie Krull's book *Fractured Grace* is about self-healing and her work includes sponsoring *Grace Circles*— *"You are invited to step outside of fear and anxiety and create beauty, peace and healing for yourself and the world."* In addition to working with *Prosocial World*, we will be connecting with multiple other networks: the Interspirituality Network (*Synergy Circles*—Kurt Johnson and Deborah Moldow), with the World Unity Network, Humanity Rising, of course Prosocial World and too many others to mention. All of these relationships are resources for your own self-empowerment.

Shared wisdom is the 'pebble' dropped into the pond of community that will change our communities the same way Nature does, holistically. When shared wisdom is passed from Circle to community it is the catalyst for change in that community. When it is shared from local-to-global instantaneously, the feedback loops create continuous and immediate improvements. The holistic spread of shared wisdom produces societal change at a scale never before imagined.

In a world that is focused on the wellbeing of the community, *community reputation* becomes the highest status an individual can hope to achieve. You can start building yours right now. Start thinking of yourself as a caretaker for all that exists in your neighborhood. You will find that as you care for your commons and the people you share it with, your commons will care for you. Little things count. Picking up the random trash. Daily greetings. Plant a garden even if it is the size of a handkerchief. I can assure you; it will make a big difference to your heart, soul, and attitude. Talk with your neighbors. Commit acts of kindness all around.

## 2. Humanity's Rite of Passage

It may seem a bit fantastic to be writing about peace, happiness and serenity in this period of incredible chaos, massive climate change, repetitive pandemics, erosion of cultural values, the rise of war and authoritarianism, the loss of trust and confidence in civil society—but NOW! is precisely the right time. I only wish that I could have written this book sooner, but that is not how it has worked for me. The timing and the inspiration come in bits and pieces and the full picture emerges in a time frame that I am not privileged to understand.

Crisis periods are short-lived. This is why I predict the saeculum ends by 2026. The near and long-term future of humanity will be determined by individual and collective choices. If you listen to most of the 'talking heads' of conventional wisdom, you will get conventional thinking. The U.S. has been the dominant nation in the world since 1946. As the global leader of the world in this last saeculum it is entirely rational to expect it to experience breaking apart and also likely to be an early leader in this collapse. When the winds of secession arise as a result of the disputed midterm elections of 2022 and 2024 in the U.S. the unravelling is quick. The same old power-*over* culture characterized by the rise of fascism, autocracy, racism, inequality will seek to impose its will on others. But like in the Rabbi's Gift or the story of The Spoons, when we learn the simple 'code' of how to care for each other, we are free to choose our own future. Nourishing each other at the scale of the individual, the community, and humankind in heart, spirit and body—is, by its very nature, only possible through power-*with*.

You don't have to accept my vision or my proposition, but two things are certain: *change is coming, and inaction will result in a no-win situation.* That means the growth greed capitalists and the politicians who back them will lose along with all the rest of us. They believe, wrongly, that they will be immune from climate disaster, immune from collapse, immune from pain and suffering. They are wrong.

As Duane Elgin pointed out in *The Promise Ahead*, this is like getting through adolescence. Humans are capable of doing this. Unfortunately, our 'leaders' are not. For most of humanity's existence, revolution has typically involved one power-*over* force being replaced by a new power-*over* force. Today, that aggressive power-*over* struggle will result in extinction or unbelievable suffering. Truthfully, it must be said that this is the direction in which we are headed <u>unless</u> <u>we</u> retake control of our shared destiny.

The autocrats of the new American fascist movement will try to exert their power-*over* all Americans, but most Americans don't want to live under tyranny. And so, the collapse of the beacon of democracy will be a prominent feature of the rising tide of autocracy globally. Many will believe that the democratic institutions they grew up with are the model for the next era because they seemed to work better than autocracies. The reality is that neither of these forms of government will survive the macroshift as they both rely on power-*over* and both result in benefiting the few. The third option is to reject both of these choices and choose an egalitarian, holistic approach that vests power in the individual and communities, based on power-*with*, and ushers in an entirely new society that exists in right relationship to the planet upon which our lives depend. I don't think this is a difficult choice.

However, for any number of reasons, it would be understandable if the vast majority of people in this world remained on the sidelines, but change doesn't just happen if *everybody* engages. Change happens when *enough people,* using the right strategies, make change happen. We know that complex systems react to fluctuations and that it only takes a relatively small number of fluctuations to create a 'tipping point'— typically 20% of the total. (See Resources <u>www.forthegoodofallnow.org</u> -The Tipping Point—Malcolm Gladwell.) We also know that in times of chaos even small fluctuations have outsized effects on the system. In terms of humanity, I calculate that, using the 8 billion people on the planet today, we need less than 1.7 billion people (20%) to co-create the *holos* fluctuation and the emergence of a brilliant new future for all. Naturally, this is a moving target. Global population is likely to decrease during the Great Turning as we struggle to reverse the impacts of polluting our home planet. Rabbi Hillel the Elder, about 2200 years ago, is credited with the expression *"If not now, when? If not you, who?"*

We know that our species has an incredibly strong history of evolutionary adaptation. This bodes well, but there is no time to waste. For your own sake and for the sake of humankind, please act NOW! The personal and societal outcomes for succeeding are almost beyond comprehension. Your cost for reimagining your life's priorities will result in personal rewards that are as magnificent as the building of *Our Lady of Unity and Peace* in the Bekaa Valley, and they will ripple out from every community. While For the Good of All, NOW! proposes a simple strategy within most people's grasp, the loss of self-belief, which hierarchy depends on to subjugate passion and reason, results in paralysis, inertia, indecision, indifference. An appalling, mind-numbing sense that nothing we do will matter. This is not true, everything matters, *"everything has a purpose,"* and as Dame Kim Conrad put so beautifully:

"What if, a polarized world were a thing of the past
Now we have the ability to live Whole at last.
To live whole because we're starting to see
We are all part of Unity.
Miracles await us as we begin to soar
Flying past boundaries that estranged us before."

The stakes at this moment of history are higher than they have ever been in the evolution of Homo sapiens on this planet! So, it is now up to each of us to declare what we are 'for'. On the one hand death and suffering on an unimaginable scale or life, unity and peace. Even as you consider all that is written here, know that your thoughts, intentions, resources, are already making waves. Let this be your springboard to take your life to the next level.

## 3. The Fourth Macroshift—*Holos*

This is not the first civilization to collapse in the history of humanity, but if we allow it to happen, it could be the extinction of Homo *sapiens*. The big event that is causing the collapse of eurocentrism, nationalism, globalization, greed-growth-capitalism and the rise of violence everywhere, is climate change. But the fact that we are talking about the possibility of extinction should raise serious questions. The *collapse* of a nation or even a civilization -like eurocentrism—is not necessarily the end of the world. But climate change unfolds on an entirely different scale: it is global and will affect every living plant and creature, every nation, every institution, every organization, every religion, every culture, every society, every person. Many casually believe that the 'leaders' will keep their focus on our safety, our future, and our wellbeing. They won't. I am writing this book because *without* understanding what *We the People* are truly capable of, it is easier to imagine nuclear annihilation or systemic collapse rather than unity and peace.

> *Only We the People are capable of restoring common sense*
> *values, by using the ancient practices of Circle and Prosocial*
> *technologies to coexist nonviolently, by vesting power in the*
> *individual, achieving self-rule, For the Good of All.*

I hope this book helps to demonstrate that the head-in-the-sand approach will simply result in surrendering to helplessness. To deal with questions of life-or-death and the survival of the species, means admitting its presence in our lives and accepting it. Only then can we empower ourselves to join others, to gain the self-belief and the skills necessary to survive and thrive. *You are not helpless!* We *are not helpless!* Because we are the caretakers, we will rule our own communities For the Good of All, NOW! And we will co-create *One Planet - One People. Holos.*

## 4. Global to Local—Epochal Change

The invasion of Ukraine has invoked all of Jared Diamond's *"five factors that have throughout history contributed to social collapse: (i) climate change, (ii) hostile neighbors, (iii) collapse of essential trading partners, (iv) environmental problems, and (v) society's response to these four factors."* (i) Climate change is implicated because as Russia turns off the spigot of natural gas, Europe will burn more coal. The global addiction to carbon may well kill the goose that laid the golden egg of the vast stores of hydrocarbons (coal, oil, gas) that resulted in the growth experienced over the past 300 years. A growth that is wreaking havoc on our climate. (ii) Russia is a hostile neighbor. (iii) The pandemic, climate disruption, and war have created worldwide shortages and supply chain issues. (iv) Environmental problems—pollution of our air, water, and soil limit our ability to deal with the biggest human-induced environmental challenge the world has ever experienced, flirting with a potential mass extinction event. (v) Society's response has been characterized as agreeing to a plan that will achieve the least worst outcome (at COP26). The Limits to Growth program that Gaya Herington ran "depicts a collapse scenario" with the most *optimistic* scenario suggesting "that it's almost, but not yet too late for society to change course."

To continue living on Earth as if there were not a care in the world and submitting to the fatalistic posture captured in a centuries' old saying that goes "whatever will be will be" is like watching the chickens appoint the fox to guard their chicken coop. We know the inevitable outcome. If we want to avoid this fate, it is on us, that is you and me, to make smarter decisions. We are not helpless. We can create the fluctuations that are capable of changing the world. "The most intractable problem today is...the lack of belief that the future is very much in the hands of the individual." (Margaret Mead) Or, as in the song "We Are The World" written by Michael Jackson and Lionel Richie, conducted and produced by Quincy Jones, and so appropriate in this moment, from which two particular lyrics stand out: "There's a choice we're making / We're saving our own lives...Let's realize that a change can only come / When we stand together as one."

Don't judge the past too harshly; hindsight provides perfect vision; foresight requires the courage of vision. Our predecessor species would not have survived the last ice age about 20,000 years ago nor made it through the cyclic nature of ice ages occurring every 100,000 years or so, if they hadn't mastered fire over a million years ago. Everything is impermanent. "Someday, after mastering the winds, the waves, the tides and gravity, we shall harness for God the energies of love, and then, for a second time in the history of the world, man will have discovered fire." Pierre Teilhard de Chardin. If we listen carefully to de Chardin, he tells us a secret we've always known, that the 'energies of love' will equip us to survive, adapt and make the transition to oneness, *holos.* "If it is to be, it is up to me."

# Section C: *How* are *We getting there?*

## Concentration and Insight

The practice of Circle is perfect for learning the powers of concentration and insight in a safe space with others. This practice is not connected to any religion. You do not need a nun, monk, priest, imam, or rabbi to create a Circle, in fact Circle is designed to be self-lead. It may help to have someone who has some experience in Circle, but even this is not necessary. If you have taken the opportunity to review *Calling the Circle* (Christina Baldwin), you already know that a simple handout can get you started and there will be ample opportunities to get coaching through For the Good of All, NOW! resources, including Prosocial/ACT. Eventually, creating and being a part of Circle will be a practice that is taught to everyone from a young age. The power of a circle practice springs from love and compassion.

The purposes and outcomes of the Circles that are part of For the Good of All, NOW! movement are:

1. To empower individuals to develop a keen awareness of their interconnection and interdependence with all life.

2. To develop, publish, and promote the shared wisdom of their Circle to seek the Good of All in their community.

3. To understand and apply the core design principles necessary for the successful administration of self-rule.

There are many other Circles meeting for many purposes. We welcome them to join us as long as they intend to develop their shared wisdom in a manner that is consistent with For the Good of All, NOW!

**The Power of Concentration/Focus:** By having the self-belief to engage in a regular practice, you become deeply mindful of the world as it truly is, impermanent (constantly changing), with positive and negative aspects, and the focused energy to, as Thich Nhat Hahn wrote, "Live in the moment...to come back to ourselves, to be alive and truly happy." Now, "When you drink your tea, just drink your tea." You will find your mind wandering less into worry, suffering, regret, or your 'To do List.' Find moments during your day to breathe deeply, even a minute will refresh you. Mindfulness leads to the power of concentration, which goes deeper and lasts longer such as preparing a meal, making a cup of tea, gazing for a sustained period at a tree or flower. This is seeing "deeply the nature of what is there." It is particularly relevant in times of *chaos*.

*When you realize how impermanent everything is,*
*the NOW becomes a source of energy.*

There is plenty to concentrate on, suffering, happiness, impermanence, interconnection, interbeing—the non-self "when you no longer see a distinction between you and your daughter or son, your anger will vanish...we can act with this kind of wisdom only after we achieve the insight of non-self." When you are mindful and your concentration comes easily, you are not deceived into ignorance about yourself and others. In Circle, when we hear the suffering or joy of others, we feel them in ourselves, without judgment—it *is* what it *is*. It requires no fixing, no effusive sympathy, just our attention, our compassionate listening and hearing. Now, when you find yourself in a power struggle, rather than anger or hate, you find something to be compassionate about—you suffer with and you experience non-self. As we experience how all earthly creations are connected and temporary, that suffering exists in us and in others and that when we inflict suffering and violence on others, we are inflicting suffering on ourselves, we fully grasp our shared fates. Shared fates are the springboard to the formation of shared values. As long as the values seek the common good, the wellbeing of all—meaning all of nature, which includes us—no one and nothing is left behind.

**The Power of Insight:** The fifth and final power is the power of insight. It is the culmination of all the powers, it "cuts through all kinds of suffering, including fear, despair anger, and discrimination." The power of self-faith, practice, mindfulness, and concentration support the power of insight. When we begin to "touch insight, we are deeply in touch with reality and there is no longer any fear. There is compassion. There is acceptance. There is tolerance...and with insight comes a tremendous source of happiness." If there is an easier or better way of reaching this level of peace, happiness, and serenity, than the practice of Circle, I am not aware of it.

Archimedes, a prolific scientist, engineer, and mathematician, who lived in the 2nd century BCE, exclaimed "Eureka!" (I've got it) after he formulated the hydrostatic principle known as the Archimedes Screw which solved the problem of moving water uphill. It would be very easy to be awed into inaction by the sheer scope of the challenges facing humanity today, kind of like making water move uphill. I think of Mikhael Rouhana, the poet-tenant farmer who, through self-belief, co-created from his heart and spirit vision, an entire new village, inspired a Pope, and built a temple to unity and peace that melted away centuries of religious hostility.

Few would argue that oneness and harmony would be harmful for our species and our planet. Oneness starts with me: when I am one with myself, fully present in body, mind, heart and spirit, I am One. This is the gateway to a much more expansive oneness that interconnects you to the Universe. I am part of a bigger, magnificent whole. Read the previous sentence again out loud. This is powerful, not difficult.

> **Getting to a tipping point that catapults us into the next paradigm, is not going to take a lot of effort by some, it will take a <u>little effort by many.</u>**

> *"... Ring the Bells that still can ring—Forget your perfect offering— There is a crack in everything—That's how the light gets in."*
> —*Anthem,* by Leonard Cohen

## Eureka! Four Turns

The following section describes the four simple steps on the path to One Planet-One People.

## I. The First Turn—Self-Empowerment

**Reward:**      Self-Actualization, Transcendence

**Means:**      Circle Practice, Right Relationship

**Accelerators:**  Power of Faith -Self-Belief; Power of Diligence—Practice

**Outcomes:**      Self-Belief, Deep Compassion—Shared Fates, Happiness, Serenity, Purpose

**Resources:**      *The Art of Power* (Thich Nhat Hanh), *Calling the Circle* (Christina Baldwin), *Fractured Grace—How to Create Beauty, Peace, and Healing For Yourself and the World* (Julie Krull)

Every turn includes a reward to spur you on, the means to propel you forward, the accelerators to quicken the pace. The outcomes become the platforms not just for a vastly richer life experience, but by providing the necessary new technologies and skill sets for the next potentially glorious stage of human evolution.

Self-actualization and transcendence make up the highest level of human realization. You graduate from a relationship where outcomes are more relevant to your life experience than the ways in which you choose to live your life. You move from striving for love, to being love, from striving for happiness, to being happy. This is a symbiotic, interdependent, cooperative relationship to life. Kabir described this state as akin to ecstasy. It occurs when we align our physical and spiritual being. It comes from practice. It comes from learning The Art of Power. It is not the exclusive realm of saints and spiritual masters, it is already in all of us, ready to be awakened.

We associate those who have reached self-actualization and transcendence with a lightness of being, a mystical spirituality, a boundless sense of peace and unity, serenity and harmony. And we think: *"Oh No, that could never be Me"*—but remember the monks in The Rabbi's Gift. Hold on to your self-belief.

We are so insulated from deep unconditional relationships, that we are often afraid to relate deeply with others, especially in more advanced economies. So, look for the *cracks* that let *the light in*. You are not alone on this path. In the company and shelter of each other in the practice of Circle, you will find true compassion by listening with your heart. As you embrace suffering, your own and the suffering of others, your life, and the lives of everyone around you will change. You will radiate an *aura*, the *aura* of oneness. The realization that you are as One, living in a temporary body and an everlasting spirit, imbued with a single source of energy—*qi*—that connects *everything*. This is the energy of power-*with*, that becomes your superpower. Awaken it through the practice of Circle.

**The First Step** is self-belief and self-empowerment through practice. It is the key to deep compassion.


## II. Second Turn—True Community

| | |
|---|---|
| **Reward**: | True Community |
| **Means:** | Circle Superpower |
| **Accelerators:** | Power of Faith - Self-Belief; Power of Diligence—Practice; + Synergy |
| **Outcomes:** | Thick *We*'s, Deep Community, Shared wisdom |
| **Resources:** | *Coming Back to Life, Practice to Reconnect Our Lives, Our World,* Joanna Macy and Molly Young Brown; *Prosocial,* by Atkins, Sloan Wilson, and Hayes |

Community today is a thin kind of community, referred to by M Scott Peck as "pseudocommunity." In a world high on cynicism and distrust, it is easy to understand why we cannot see beyond the blind spot in the mirror despite the general recognition that we are facing a level of disaster that our species has not experienced since the last Ice Age. Right relationship will erase the blind spot.

True community has always been grounded in the actions of Thick *We's* and shared fates. The conveniences of modern-day life diminish the sense of shared fates that used to bond us closely to each other which has resulted in a society of Atomized *I*'s. The perception of the supremacy of the individual is deeply embedded in the Western Eurocentric culture of the last saeculum. Atomized *I*'s will simply not survive the increasing chaos of climate disasters. The strong unity felt in a communal response to a disaster is synergy at work, a force where "one equals ten or a hundred or even a thousand!" (Stephen Covey)

Shared fates, spirit connection, the right relationship of caretaker, these are the pathways to the sense of being part of a larger clan, a community. These are the portals to co-creating true community, and they are the most important predictors of the survival of our species. True community is the light that pierces through the *cracks* of a dark future. It is the result of the synergistic action of millions of people consciously making the decision to empower themselves, each other and their communities by reconnecting through a right relationship to each other and the world as caretakers, not exploiters.

**The Second Step** is the superpower of Circle, a practice that nourishes deep community and produces the people's shared wisdom as *We the People* reclaim our commons For the Good of All, NOW!

## III. Third Turn—Self-Rule

| | |
|---|---|
| **Reward:** | Self-Rule |
| **Means:** | Shared Wisdom, Prosocial Training |
| **Accelerators:** | Power of Mindfulness, Federation of People's Committees (see Section E) |
| **Outcomes:** | more Synergy, Consensual Democracy, Prosocial Communities |
| **Resources:** | *Prosocial* (Atkins, Sloan Wilson, and Hayes) |

In *The Neighborhood Project—Using Evolution to Improve My City, One Block at a Time*, David Sloan Wilson writes: "Large-scale human society cannot be built directly from individuals. It needs to be multicellular, like a multicellular organism."

Gandhi and Jayprakash Narayan demonstrated that self-rule through community circle practices can be successful. The community circle embraces a holistic rather than hierarchical construction. It becomes the true *Voice of the People*, arrived at through discussion and consensus, not by the power-*over* of rulers and politicians, but through the power-*with* of people speaking for their community. Gandhi sets three other important rules for his world vision of self-rule: a) coexist nonviolently, b) vest power in the individual, and c) seek the good of all. Most importantly, it cannot be politicized. Party representatives are the only people who cannot join a Circle, because it is impossible to mix the oil of politics with the water of Circle. Ultimately, there will be no need for political parties and politicians, so this distinction is temporary. Future generations will look at the past and wonder—"What were they thinking?"

Achieving a vision for the world that reflects unity and peace rather than one where "the heart" is "small, and hard, and full of meanness" requires seeing the world through the lens of how change happens in natural systems rather than man-made ones. The reconsideration of the core value of power-*with*, releases us from power-*over* so essential in hierarchies. While the 'leaders' and holders of most of the wealth in this world, have a vested interest in maintaining hierarchy, their influence in our commons is weak, compared to their influence in "the corridors of power." The blind spot of thinking that power-over is the best strategy for changing power-over is avoided through a communal shared wisdom stemming from right relationship.

It is time for a massive strategic pivot to make change happen at the community level while encouraging its spread globally. If we want our communities to live in unity and peace, to pursue the wellbeing of all, then *We the People and the leaders of the movements who work so tirelessly to make unity and peace must join together and use our power-with to demand it locally.*

The Third Step does good For the Good of All, NOW! It establishes a common basis for unified action and builds on power-*with* created through, deep compassion, deep community, and Thick *We's* to regenerate self-rule For the Good of All.

## IV. Fourth Turn—Oneness

**Reward:**       Oneness

**Means:**       Circle + Prosocial

**Accelerators:** Power of Insight, The Hive—Interconnection

**Outcomes:**    Trusteeship, Interbeing, Thrival

**Resources:**    *The Web of Meaning* (Jeremy Lent)

We cannot surpass the design of nature. Mr. Lent's work, *The Web of Meaning*, is absolutely compatible with David Sloan Wilson's Prosocial World and ACT (Acceptance and Commitment Therapy) technology, The Earth Charter, and The Sixteen Indigenous Principles. We will avoid the blind spot of thinking that power-*over* is the best strategy for changing power-*over*, because we know that power-*with* is the universal force. We will embrace and practice in Circle Gandhi's vision for the world to coexist nonviolently and peacefully. We will vest power in the individual. We will seek to do good For the Good of All, NOW! Everything changes once we understand that our role is to act with a common purpose as caretakers—seeking to care for everything in creation for the benefit of ALL forever.

Future humans, if or when they reclaim the natural oneness of the physical and the spiritual, will exist in a vastly different world where the prime directive of doing good For the Good of All is connected to the health of an entire ecosystem living in balance. Exploitation of people and resources will be unimaginable to our caretaker descendants. The center of life will be community, but our co-existence across the world as One People—One Planet will fully embrace the diversity and oneness of our relationship to each other, the earth, and the universe. All will be venerated and treated as co-equals, because every task undertaken is meant For the Good of All. Harming others would be as if we were harming ourselves. When a harm is done to another, we apply the Eight Core Design Principles and ACT method to quickly restore balance and harmony. This is true for resolving individual as well as group differences from local-to-global. As we experience oneness, nature blesses us once again with bounty, which we use wisely For the Good of All.

There will still be disagreements and discussions. There will still be hills to climb and pitfalls to avoid, but shared wisdom and shared experiences will form a vital system of feedback and adjustment, constantly seeking to improve our capacity to achieve the wellbeing of each other, the community and the planet we are tending.

**The Fourth Step:** The practice of Circle combined with prosocial technologies leads to insight, self-actualization and the transcendent state of *holos*—our essential oneness. As *we practice* oneness, *we* become one.

It stands to reason that a culture that would shamelessly exploit all resources, pollute the environment so radically that it threatens the survival of the species, use war to kill other humans, and do all this for the good of the few is *absurd*. To believe that those who continue to exert power-*over* are even capable of perceiving this reality, is the Great Self-Deception. It ends when *We the People* reclaim our lives, ourselves.

# Section D: *What changes can We expect?*

| FROM | TO | OUTCOMES |
|---|---|---|
| **DEEP SELF** | | |
| Hierarchy—Power-*over* | Holarchy—Power-*with* | Oneness |
| Exploiter | Caretaker | Right Relationship |
| Greatest Value for the Few | Common Good, Wellbeing of All | For the Good of All |
| Confirmation Bias | Flexibility, Open Mind | Adaptation |
| Centralized Power | Decentralized | Synergy |
| Personal Wealth/power | Community Reputation | Self-Actualization, Transcendence |
| **DEEP COMMUNITY** | | |
| Cult of Individual, Atomized *I*'s | Power of Circle, Thick *We*'s | True Community, Interbeing |
| Individual Choice | Collective Choice | Cooperation, Collaboration |
| Capitalism/Globalization | Localism, Common Good Capitalism | Local-to-Global |
| Institutions, Organizations | 8 Core Design Principles | Prosocial World |
| Politics/Governance | Self-Rule, Web of Interbeing®, 8 CDPs | Power of Community |
| Violence | Nonviolence, Love Force | Peace, Interbeing |
| Dominance | Cooperation | Peace, Interconnection |
| Separation | Unity | Peace, Interconnection |
| Meanness | Compassion | Health, Interdependent |

| Discord | Harmony | Peace, Serenity |
|---|---|---|
| Inequity, Inequality | Fairness, equity, equality | Equitable |
| Resistance | Fluidity | Harmony |
| **DEEP CONNECTION** | | |
| Vest power at the top | Vest power at the lowest level | Subsidiarity |
| Mechanical design | Ecological Design | Efficiency, Harmony |
| Nationalism | Localism | Efficiency, Self-Rule |
| Growth | Wellbeing/sufficiency | Common Good Capitalism |
| Discord, Disunity | Unity & Peace, Egalitarianism | *Holos*—Oneness |

## 1. Localism—Sufficiency, Self-Rule, Consensual Democracy

Localism is not new. It is manifested by local production, local consumption, local government, and local culture. One of the foremost teachers and innovators in this field is my friend Michael Shuman. Again, as the world shrinks in terms of occupiable space and weakened supply chains, localism should become part of the curriculum and language wherever economics is taught and applied in every economic undertaking. The premise for localism is to stop leaking money out of the local economy, while building the wellbeing of the community (see also Resources at www.forthegoodofallnow.org for links to the *Community Wealth Building: Eight Basic Principles* at the Democracy Collaborative, a rich source of information on a variety of relevant topics; *Donut Economics*, Kate Raworth; *The Center for New Economics* [formerly the Schumacher Center for a New Economics] Susan Witt, David Bollier, et al).

"The Promise of A Million Utopias" is a document by Michael Shuman (the author of *The Small Mart Revolution, Going Local, Local Dollars Local Sense, The Local Economy Solution, Put your Money Where Your Life Is,* and more)—see Resources www.forthegoodofallnow.org) will banish any doubts about our collective ability to co-create local economies from the bottom up—subsidiarity is front and center. Though the solutions are specific to the U.S., the practices are relevant from country to country and community to community.

*Our current existential threat is <u>not</u> a failure of humanity,*
*it is a failure of humanity's design selection.*

We could have chosen egalitarianism, but we chose hierarchy; power-*over* instead of power-*with*. Localism does not preclude globalism—a system of sharing and trading goods and information with communities globally—it simply replaces globalization with ways to be more self-sufficient and to share resources equitably For the Good of All. It goes hand in hand with oneness, harmony and balance.

**This Tiny Country Feeds the World** (see Resources at www.forthegoodofall.org). This article appeared in the September 2017 *National Geographic* Magazine (recommended to all readers along with Yes! Magazine). Here we are in 2022 having done little to adapt to the coming crises related to the global availability and production of food, while we face certain shortages in wheat from Ukraine and Russia. Meanwhile, the Dutch are the second largest exporter of food in the world (based on value) after the U.S. The U.S. covers 9.8 million square kilometers, Holland just under 7,500 square kilometers. The U.S. population is over 331.5 million, Holland's population is almost 6.6 million. We can learn how to feed ourselves locally and feed the world. Communities can collaborate to rationalize production and trade between themselves, while building a hedge against climate change and shortening supply chains and its inevitable disruptions. This holistic design provides greater resilience and efficiency to trade for that which we can't produce locally. This may not be the kind of back to the land movement many are familiar with, but it would work well as part of a community-supported agriculture program, and it will be necessary. It reminds me of a project called Growing Power that Will Allen (MacArthur Foundation Genius Grant recipient) launched in Milwaukee. It ran into some problems after 20 years mostly related to the challenges of operating as a non-profit under U.S. law. His advice remains that the model wasn't the problem. The problem lies with the complicated ways entrepreneurs need to finance community benefit operations. I highly recommend that communities develop a local agriculture program and revisit the Growing Power model. Michael Shuman has developed a wealth of knowledge and advice on how to build local economies.

Localism, self-rule, consensual democracy and the reclaiming of our Commons will happen because they can and will replace the old unsustainable systems that separated us from our natural state of oneness. There is very little that needs to be invented. There are programs operating now that can be reproduced anywhere.

## 2. The Commons, The Uncommons and The Great Awakening

The uncommons are categories that do not fit well in our understanding of the commons, either as a result of scale, scope or relationships. Professor Johnathon B. Wiener at Duke University uses the term to group the kinds of risks that are so *uncommon*, either in occurrence or scope that different strategies and rules apply to them. These consist of mega-risks, like a meteor hit; or low frequency but big change risks, like pandemics, climate change, world wars; and, at the lowest end in terms of scope, though not necessarily frequency, tsunamis, raging wildfires, contamination from extra-terrestrial materials.

Professor Shoshana Zuboff (*The Age of Surveillance Capitalism*) at Harvard University refers to the *un-commons* as the human information data that we produce. In a modern-day twist on colonialism, the tech giants—Google, Facebook (now Meta), Microsoft, Apple—are colonialists mining, extracting, and misappropriating and benefiting from our personal data without our explicit knowledge, consent, or compensation. These huge corporate entities are answerable to no one. The purpose of these enterprises is to extract the greatest value for the Few at the expense of All by creating special rights and interests that deflect responsibility for the excessive damage left in their wake. Our privacy is just another rich mineral vein to be mined by capitalists. The political 'leaders,' under much public pressure, may tweak the *status quo*, but they won't challenge the very premise that our personal data belongs to us, because they are beholden to the elites and corporations who finance their political parties and campaigns. This is not new, think— oil, gas, air and airwaves, wind, water—anything that can be used to create wealth for the wealthy is fair game and it is done with the full support of the ruling classes and politicians. In *Democracy in America,* Alexis de Tocqueville (1835) wrote: "There are many men of principle in both parties in America, but there is no party of principle." These 'leaders' and elites deny any responsibility for the destruction of what people hold dear—our privacy—and the broader impacts this loss of the personal right to privacy takes on culture and society. The idea of the 'uncommons' challenges us to think beyond Hardin's meadow analogy to a commons that includes late-capitalist tech enterprises. In other words, it makes sense to expand our understanding of the commons to include human and non-human aspects that are integral to the whole of life.

In *The Great Awakening—New Modes of Life Amidst Capitalist Ruins,* Anna Grear and David Bollier, the editors Grear and Bollier present a series of academic papers from leading edge thinkers about how "commoning will change politics, governance, and indeed the nation-state." David

Bollier is the Schumacher Center's Reinventing the Commons Program Director and Anna Grear is the Founder and Editor-in-Chief of the Journal of Human Rights and the Environment, and one of the luminaries in the work relating to human rights and the environment. They suggest that "the commons…is also an archetypal form of biomaterial intelligence that emerges from within the blasted landscapes of capitalist ruins." David Bollier on his website http://www.bollier.org describes the richness of the commons and why it is not just about economics. He writes:

"I should perhaps interject here that a commons is not a resource in itself. It's a resource *plus* a social community *and* the social values, rules and norms that they used to manage the resource. They're all an integrated package.  Call it a socio-economic-biophysical package, sort of like a fish and a pond and aquatic vegetation: They all go together and don't make sense as isolated parts."

These four attributes of the commons form the interconnection of the physical and spiritual dimensions which Joni Mitchell sang about at Woodstock in 'We Are Stardust'—where the small reflects the large and the health of the whole ecosystem depends on the health of each part. These qualities of the commons are consistent with Jeremy Lent's principles of ecological design. Grear and Bollier suggest: "Forms of commoning do not look to magic blueprints for change, but rather to demonstrated patterns and norms that allow people to build new sorts of institutions grounded in their actual needs and where they actually live in a human-nonhuman knot of connections. In short, commoning offers a compelling evolutionary strategy for escaping some structural dead-ends in which humanity now finds itself entrapped." This could also describe self-rule For the Good of All.

We are destined to either regain our superpower of deep compassion, re-awaken deep community, achieve deep connection and the insight to wield the Eight Core Design Principles, or choose to "Be For" a mass suicidal group indifference to our fate. Neither national governments, nor tech giants, nor corporations, nor international organizations, have demonstrated that they can enter into right relationship, give up power-*over* and become caretakers For the Good of All, NOW! Who will assume this role? You and I, and billions of others will. Our shared mission is to manage our commons. Future generations, if there are any and I firmly believe there will be, will wonder 'What were they thinking?'

> "Ring the bells that still can ring
> Forget your perfect offering
> There is a crack, a crack in everything
> That's how the light gets in."
> From *Anthem* by Leonard Cohen

## 3. Common Good Capitalism—Consensual Wealth

The Co-Founder of Common Good Capitalism, Terry Mollner, the one whose two articles changed my life, has a new book: *Common Good Capitalism is Inevitable.* (See Resources at www.forthegoodofallnow. org.)

**Common Good Capitalism** essentially seeks to establish a cooperatively competitive business marketplace, large and small, between businesses that choose as their highest priority the common good first, and mission or profit second. Common good capitalism contains Gandhi's concepts of the common good and trusteeship. Capitalism leaves a sour taste in many mouths because it exploits and abuses the majority, while reserving all the benefits for a few but this is what it became. Capital will still be required to build strong communities. Robert Putnam introduced us to social capital which has been expanded to include seven more forms of capital described by Wealthworks.org as: Individual, Intellectual, Social, Cultural, Natural, Built, Political, in addition to Financial.

(https://www.wealthworks.org/basics/explore-regional-wealth-building/wealth-eight-capitals). The concepts and vision that Terry Mollner and his team describe are those of a ground-breaking entrepreneur deeply steeped in the realities and the vision of Gandhi. This, and commoning, and Localism, are the kinds of experiences and knowledge that will guide us through to the next iteration of capitalism.

**Capital:** There will always be a need for capital to create and sustain businesses. Localism is a way to keep that capital in the community. Wealth, like everything in a world of oneness, is multicellular. My vision of a *consensual wealth* system is that it would emulate *consensual democracy*. At the community level, for example, a Community Chest could be set up to accept capital in the form of investments or donations. The Community Chest becomes the lender or investor of choice for local enterprises and would pay dividends or interest to the local investors. Like the people's committees, the Community Chests would spread in ever-widening circles of communities until they cover the entire planet. Local currencies will proliferate. The purpose of the use of capital will be to improve the wellbeing of all in that community. Many businesses will be organized as cooperatives or owned by the employees as stockholders, or Community Benefit Corporations.

**Organizations:** The Eight Core Design Principles and ACT will become the operating system for *all* groups, including businesses, allowing for an exciting new springboard for innovation harnessed to producing the good of all. All the inefficiencies and distortions of hierarchy are replaced in a nature-based holistic system sustained by instantaneous feedback loops. Once rid of its many layers, trade between communities can be simplified and facilitated using current technology that will only get better at minimizing complexity. The new-found power-*with* of organizations will co-create the common good. Though the world may become less complex, it will not be going backwards. Common Good Capitalism is very much aligned with Gandhi's work, no surprise there, and its association with Terry Mollner assures me that it is a genuine and well-thought out project for the *holos macroshift.*

## 4. The Path Ahead

Every Fourth Turning since 1485 has ended violently. The Turning that began in 1946 fits the pattern of saecular turnings, but it is playing out in a civilizational *macroshift* that includes the chaos of climate change.

We are quite visibly in the throes of an unwinding catastrophe of our own making based on greed-growth-capitalism. The imminent break-up of the world's leading democracy for the last 150 years is symbolic of the failure of thinking that bigger is better. In the seeds of destruction, it is possible to see the green shoots of a new world. We see that *The Emperor Has No Clothes* and this awareness helps to ignite a healing process. The new world vision is centered on the evolutionary transition to oneness and a new Prosocial/ACT operating system for humanity committed to achieving the wellbeing of both people and nature. Our relationships to each other and our environment will shift as the practice of oneness begets oneness. The operating systems for humanity are vastly improved. Human relations take a giant leap. Communities operate independently but are closely knitted and self-governing. The vision for our future is optimistic because the shared fate of Homo *sapiens* is its ability to adapt wisely. However, I have to admit that there is great cause for concern. The apocalyptic—dystopian—perspectives of many artists, from the Mad Max movies to zombie apocalypses, and Margaret Atwood's *The Handmaid's* Tale, among many others, confirm that the transition is going to be challenging. Hopefully, the dramatic slowdown in economic activity as a result of chaos will be one of the most welcomed adaptive processes as it will slow down the rate and intensity of climate change and provide us with the room to regroup and restore a more friendly and benevolent interrelationship with our climate. I believe we will avoid total collapse, but it will only be realized by people understanding their power and acting on it For the Good of All, NOW! Some believe it will happen in a generation, others perceive a longer period of adaptation. The fact is: it depends on us.

In the very short term, the turbulence will result in a rapid collapse. I suppose the most obvious and talked about collapse will occur in the economy, which is already being spoken about in apocalyptic terms, and why not. We have been furiously printing money to prop up the engines of wealth that make the élites in the business and political world go round. This house of cards is all connected. We are witnessing the collapse of the institutions of democracy, justice, politics, and civil society all at the same time. New institutions will rise from the ashes and prime among them will be self-rule. Even so, there is a stubborn insistence that the iceberg in front of us will never sink the ship, and so the band plays on. As the world burns, literally and figuratively, it has become ever more clear that the people must engage and seek the change they want to see in the world. As Gandhi told us: "If we could change ourselves, the tendencies in the world would also change. As a man changes his own nature, so does the attitude of the world change towards him."

I take comfort in the words of Strauss and Howe: "Come the fourth turning, in the white heat of society's... rebirth, a grand solution may suddenly snap into place." They made a prediction twenty-five years ago that this saeculum would end in 2025—Pretty impressive! I admit that in the first drafts of this book, I extended the end out to the mid-2030s as I hoped for more lead time to prepare. The war in Ukraine shattered that illusion. Nevertheless, I am optimistic because I see the growing shift of humanity around us, and it will only grow larger and more effective as the situation deteriorates. The path described here will not succeed through an enormous sacrifice on the part of a few. That is a recipe for disaster. It will only succeed when a sufficient mass of individuals makes a personal commitment to engage with the world differently. All the tools and actions necessary for a successful passage are within the grasp of every person willing to take the step. Together, power-*with* will become the change we want to see.

## 5. Resilience

Crisis periods are short-lived. This is why I predict the saeculum ends by 2026. The future of humanity will be determined by individual and collective choices, NOW! If you listen to most of the 'talking heads' of 'conventional wisdom', you will get conventional thinking. As the global leader in this last saeculum it is entirely rational to expect that the U.S. will be the most affected in the unfolding *macroshift*, quickly joined by all the economic superpowers. The same old power-*over* culture characterized by the *current* rise of fascism, autocracy, racism, inequality will quickly collapse, just as it always has. As in the story of The Spoons, when we learn the simple 'code' of how to care for each other life wins. Nourishing each other at scale, meaning globally in heart, spirit and body, by its very nature, is only possible through power-*with*.

Yet we persist in thinking that the future is going to resemble the past. This is normal. This is a mind-trick referred to as *confirmation bias*. It is quite natural to process incoming information in the context of our existing beliefs and expectations. A perfect example at this moment in time, is the *confirmation bias* among many White people that there is some kind of global conspiracy to replace them. No matter how absurd such a claim is, increasingly bizarre claims are circulated to confirm the bias that the White race is being replaced. As this fits their predetermined world view, any information that confirms their bias is embraced.

The reality is quite different. The reality is that White Eurocentric power-*over*, which spread its virus globally, is about to be replaced by power-*with*, an equally invasive but beneficial bacterium. Though we intuitively and scientifically know that power-*with* produces synergy, we are still conditioned by *confirmation bias* that power-*over* will prevail. It is time to let that delusion go.

In addition to the wisdom of L A Paul and Pema Chödrön, the American Psychological Association suggests a roadmap for "adapting to life-changing situations" that will sound very familiar to you: "<u>Build Your Connections</u>—prioritize relationships...join a group...; <u>Foster Wellness</u>—practice mindfulness manage stress, rather than seeking to eliminate the feeling of stress...; <u>Find Purpose</u>—help others...be proactive...move toward your goals...look for opportunities for self-discovery...; <u>Embrace Healthy Thoughts</u>—keep things in perspective...accept change...maintain a hopeful outlook." (<u>https://www.apa.org/topics/resilience/building-your-resilience</u>).

## 6. Call to Action

Today we live in a time of self-made climate change, at a time of incredible technological breakthroughs in terms of communication and connectivity, the most serious threat of nuclear war since the 1962 Cuban missile crisis, while observing the same drift towards grievance-driven autocracy that occurred just before WWII. I suspect most of humanity is coming around to the reality that has been with us since the bombing of Hiroshima and Nagasaki in 1945. Namely, that we have the capability to destroy ourselves. Whether we accomplish self-annihilation through war or we fail to adapt to climate change, or Western civilization spins out of control, or a combination of these and other factors, the end result is clear: if power-*over* prevails, there will be no winners. And this is important, while autocrats may be celebrating the many challenges facing Western style democracy, they are completely ignoring their own need to reassess their failures and stresses. The rigidity of autocracy makes it much more vulnerable to collapse, and sadly their citizens are going to be more adversely affected and will have less power to shape their futures than the more flexible and resilient democracies. Because even if they have been weakened, there is an embedded culture built on the concept of the *Voice of the People*. And as Gandhi wrote: tyrants always fall.

None of us would likely choose to be involved in a macroshift, but we were born into a cycle that places us here now. As described in great detail in *The Fourth Turning,* every generation has a role to play in this time of transition. Strauss and Howe predict how this turning of the wheel is consistent with the previous 26 turnings going back to ancient Rome. There is great comfort to be learned from these cycles of history. Likewise, the stories that describe the human condition, our myths, provide us with a deeper understanding of our inner strength and beauty. Joseph Campbell (*The Power of Myth*) wrote that there are two types of myths—the story of a physical deed where the hero "performs a courageous act...or saves a life" and a spiritual deed where the hero experiences "the supernatural range of human spiritual life and then comes back with the message." We are all capable of courageous acts and performing spiritual feats.

*We are physical and spiritual beings deeply interconnected*
*as one and inseparable from the web of all life. It is our*
*responsibility and great privilege to become caretakers of*
*each other and our world.*

Everyone has a role to play. Borrowing from the wisdom of Strauss and Howe's *The Fourth Turning* and in their style, here are my messages for each of the generations alive today:

**Dear Elder,** (63 years +) Imagine all your planning and hopes for those comfortable golden years leading you into the hereafter turned upside down by what Strauss and Howe refer to as the *Great Devaluation*. Whatever wealth you had, it is now of no value. The only real value is your community reputation. You can be bitter, if you choose to be, but as an old Greek proverb goes: *"**A society grows great when old men plant trees whose shade they know they shall never sit in.**"*

Become part of the solution by rejecting the power-*over* culture we have known our entire lives, and which threatens our descendants with extinction. Our work is not done. Our lives will become hugely purposeful as the custodian-grandparents we are. Many are in positions of leadership; it is time to reframe your purpose. Let's start planting trees both figuratively and literally. I invite you to join me and billions of others.

**Dear Midlifer,** (42-62) You are likely to either lean towards being a strong supporter of creating communities of purpose, or toward authoritarianism by ordering others to do your bidding. You have played by the rules all your life and you expect your rewards. But they've been snatched from you. You are the group that will determine the future of human society so your actions are the ones that will largely shape the ultimate outcome. The Power of Circle will be a big step for you. Strange to you at first, some of you will soon gain strength and power you never knew you had. Circle will help you understand how to wield power-*with*, with love and compassion. You already share deep love and compassion for the young, tap into this common trait For the Good of All, NOW!

**Dear Young Adult,** (21-41) You see the world of your grandparents and parents in shambles. You have long been accustomed to seeking your own counsel, even if it often revolved around video-game depictions of real life. You are likely to seek advice from the Elders and figure out what to do with the help of the Midlifers, but be very careful of your tendency to want to impose order (power-*over*) on a world that is in chaos. My biggest hope for you and those who look up to you, the children, is that you find your own wisdom gifts in Circle. Remember your new role as a caretaker. It will serve as your touchstone. You are being catapulted into a highly charged situation that you have had no say over. Now is the time to speak up. Push your parents and grandparents. Be an example to the children. You are more open to new experiences and you are thinking a lot about whether your life will include even a shot at self-actualization and transcendence (BTW: you always have that opportunity and it materializes as oneness not fame, popularity, or money!) The biggest challenge ahead of you is to co-develop the particular shared wisdom that comes, not necessarily from personal experience, but from shared experiences—good and bad. This is made easier as you understand power-*with* and power-*over*, how *shared fates* provide you the gift of deep community. The old practice of Circle is your source of a new power to attain shared wisdom and love. Given that I am certain humanity will make it through this transition period, you and the children who follow you will be making the decisions that will shape the new world. Your reward will come in your lifetime, and it will come through the power of Circle. *Carpe diem*. Seize the day!

**Dear Children,** (0-20) You are the children of the turning. You will grow up at a time of great upheaval. It will be new to you, as everything is new. You will grow up being taught new norms and customs. Circle practice will be as normal to you as grasping new technologies was to the Young Adults you look up to now. You will have known a world in chaos struggling to survive and you will come to terms with the new reality. You will never forget your powerlessness and fear, but also how protected and precious you were to your elders. You will grow up knowing your integral, indivisible, oneness with all life on Earth. You will grow up with the practices of Circle. You will absorb the art of power-*with* and the prime directive to do good for the good of all, without even understanding the full meaning of these words today. The lingering chaos and humanity's mythic passage will be the stories you tell your grandchildren.

## 7. Joint Ventures

I recommend revisiting the few paragraphs in Chapter 2 related to Gaya Herington's work on the Limits to Growth in The Journal of Industrial Ecology (2021) and Jim Collins's and *How the Mighty Fall* as preparatory work. (Links to these are found in Resources at www.forthegoofofallnow.org.) A joint venture is quite simply an agreement to collaborate on a project in a way that makes a shared desired outcome easier to achieve while using fewer resources to do it. You are more likely to solve complex problems collaboratively than by yourself. Teams accomplish more than individuals. Many hands make light work, as the saying goes. Synergy is a superpower. A joint venture is not a thinly disguised plot to gain an advantage, it is a mutually beneficial partnership. It is not a competition. It is a collaboration.

> **Dear Organization Leaders,** Hierarchy is terribly inefficient. Holism is the model of the most complex system we know, and it is tremendously efficient, though not perfect, we call it nature. Whether your organization is intended to do good or to make a profit, it seems to me you would want to be as efficient as possible. Likewise, power-*with* is more efficient (and natural) than power-*over*. I respectfully suggest that NOW might be a good time to *engage in long-term planning and reconsider core values*. Patagonia has been a leader in this regard, but there are many others. Accepting the challenge to become good caretakers (trustees) doing good For the Good of All brings a new sense of value and *values* to your mission work. If you are a for-profit organization now, you may want to consider your options—community benefit corporation, trusteeship, or you can remain for-profit, but do it for the good of all, and you will measure your success in entirely new ways. Imagine for a second, that all the disguises have been laid bare —The Emperor Has No Clothes—will you or your organization be seen as an exploiter of resources and people to benefit the few, be able to compete successfully in the new paradigm, while hundreds

of smaller more nimble competitors, committed to nurturing resources and people, are delivering products and services that are safer and better for everyone, while promoting the common good? They innovate better. They are better at every level of organization because they have removed the levels. They are now working as a superorganism. Are you prepared to compete against this kind of highly productive, super-efficient organization? Are you ready for a world where the focus is local not global? And if your service or product has global application, is it contributing to the good of all? No doubt we will still need systems to bridge, and connect across the world, but these connections will look and serve vastly different purposes than the ones we have now.

**Dear Movement Leaders,** If you want to grow your sphere of influence and your impact the quickest most efficient way to do it is through joint ventures to work with other organizations in a coordinated effort, to organize your enterprise and your movement to co-create Circles at the local level, and to support and uplift the local Circles to seek change locally. Let this become your new buzz word. Who can you reach out to today to begin forging a mutually beneficial relationship? This is how multicellular networks are designed. We are all too aware of the duplication of effort and work that exists in the not-for-profit sector. What I am saying is neither original nor revelational. What causes us to pause is the fear of losing control. Power-*over* is deeply entrenched even in the minds of those who believe in power-*with*. The pull of hierarchy creates a powerful *confirmation bias* in leaders that there are only leaders and followers, that if people and groups aren't managed, controlled and supervised they'll go off the rails. I urge you to reconsider. Join a Prosocial/ACT twelve-week generation cycle as an introduction or take the full course, yourself or as a management team. It will take approximately 24 to 48 hours over 12 weeks to become sufficiently acquainted with the power of this practice. This will change your relationship to your people, your volunteers, your customers, your supporters and to the fulfillment of your vision and mission. There is hardly a moment to spare. The future looks very different NOW. In most businesses, two to four years represents a long time, are you preparing now for a future that looks very different. Remember Gaya Herrington's conclusions that there is but a sliver of hope of avoiding collapse. This will require new vision and clarity, are you preparing yourself and your movement. Your community reputation will be vastly more important than your status as a corporate leader. Your organization is a synergistic community, tap into this power-*with.*

Empower individuals in your movement to work in Circles, and they will make change at a whole new level. This is called subsidiarity. It is the way nature works. Innovation, collaboration, synergy, will begin to flow. You are now truly guiding and nurturing your teams to co-create great music. There is one caveat; if you or your organization are using power-*over* strategies, you will have defeated yourselves. Don't even try it. Rather, immediately implement a true power-*with* set of core values as part of your planning.

Of all the leaders in all the different kinds of organizations, surely you understand the interconnectedness of the human superorganism. As a leader, speak with other leaders. If you are an activist working with others to make change happen, organize yourselves as Circles. Watch in amazement as the power of community through Circle arises. An anti-hunger or a peace advocate is also likely to be concerned about poverty, inequality, climate change, and any number of other issues. Imagine the effects of self-empowered Circles in your community joining together to develop shared wisdom that crosses all the lines, because in reality there are no separating lines in a commons. Soon, you realize what has been true all along "Never doubt that a small group of thoughtful, committed, citizens can change the world. Indeed, it is the only thing that ever has."

You've devoted a lot of time and energy assessing your competitive strengths and weaknesses and those of your competitors or allies. This is easy, pick up the phone and propose ways to help each other do more, by finding joint venturing and co-managing opportunities to accomplish more For the Good of All.

But know this, if your purpose is to extract and plunder, none of these strategies will work: no joint venture, no caretaker ethos, no benefits of synergy and holism will work using power-*over*. The Good of the Few is over. The longer it lingers in our midst the longer the transition lasts. Just like Dame Conrad asks us as individuals what you are for, you must ask these same questions: what is your organization for? If it is to make profits for the few, are you are prepared to adapt? Let the holistic system of life, a multi-cellular system work holistically. If you rise to the occasion, a phoenix is ready to rise with you, even in the midst of a collapse, especially in the midst of a collapse. Nothing can stop a united and strategic power-*with* effort to do good For the Good of All, NOW! I suggest that this is the only scenario that gets us beyond the collapse of the Limits to Growth.

**Special Note to Religious Leaders:** Most religious institutions grew out of the *theos* macroshift which gave birth to your institution. I am not a theologian, but I do know that most religious institutions honor the spirit that imbues all life. I humbly suggest that many of your religious movements started in Circle and recognized the divine spark of energy in all of us. Yours is possibly the most difficult or the easiest of transitions. Teilhard de Chardin's vision of oneness occurring at the Omega Point is an eschatological—end of times—event. I rather perceive it as a moment to take a huge step closer to our Spirit selves, something many successful religious teachers already try very hard to accomplish. The world is changing in many miraculous ways, at least I hope so. The evolutionary transition that seeks the Good of All, should include religious institutions.

**To all** who have been trying to organize the millions of people and groups seeking change, I hope For the Good of All, NOW! presents a new super-tool and strategy for your work be it climate, race, poverty, peace, equality, justice, etc. I hope that the levers of an overarching goal—For the Good of All, NOW!—and the significance of the Prosocial-ACT technology will, when combined with the radical shift in strategy to work from the bottom up rather than the top down, ignite in you the inspiration and passion to impassion your people through Circle to seek change in their communities. This is practical and replicable in every community and organization. It will drive you and your supporters to join with others—individuals, groups, organizations. The cells, the Circles, represent new power-*with* centers that will make your job of coordination a deep pleasure instead of a worry. These resulting changes and interconnections are, I am sure you would agree, impossible unless we embrace these new/old design systems. Let us form a global joint venture to *interconnect* For the Good of All, NOW! The time is coming.

## 8. One Billion Starfish, NOW!

It takes 2 people each asking 2 other people to join your Circle. Then those 2 people get 2 more people involved. Do this 30 times and it will add up to 1 billion Circle co-creators! How long it takes will depend on decisions made by people like you, people you know, people you don't, all coming together and declaring What You Are For. There is a well-known story used by fundraisers called the Starfish Story.

A young man is walking along a beach. The sea has washed up millions of starfish who are stranded and dying on the beach. As he walks, he stoops down, picks up a starfish and throws it back in the ocean.

As he is walking, an older man coming from the opposite direction approaches. The old man stops the young man and asks him what he's doing. The young man says: *"If I don't throw them back in, they'll die.*" To which the older man replies, "*But what difference can it make, there are starfish as far as the eye can see.*" The young man replies: "*It makes a difference to this one,*" as he tosses a starfish back in the sea.

This was meant to encourage donors to make a difference and donate to the fundraiser's cause. More subtly, it also had the negative effect of highlighting the capriciousness of using random acts of kindness to achieve the common good, instead of building out proper strategies. Do not misinterpret my meaning: Please do as many random acts of kindness as you can. Doing good For the Good of All, NOW! connects seemingly random acts into a potent organized force that shows, without arguing, without rancor, without protest, without violence, how every Circle and every community can use power-*with* to open a pathway to self-governance by sharing their wisdom throughout the community and asking the questions Rabbi Hillel asked: "If I am not for myself, then who will be for me? And if I am for myself only, then what am I? And if not now, when?"

It will not be lost on many environmentalists that there is another starfish story, one that makes this story all the more poignant in our time. In 1969, the ecologist Robert Paine discovered that when starfish disappeared from a reef, the reef ecosystem would collapse. Subsequent research over the years has confirmed this phenomenon and more keystone species get added to the list as more ecosystems collapse. It is likely you already know some of them: pollinator bees, sharks, lions, wolves, even mangrove trees and enough other examples for some to compare this time to the Sixth Mass Extinction. The starfish story is important for reasons well beyond fundraising!

We will get through the Great Turning because the new paradigm results from reaching for the stardust within each of us, reaching through the '*cracks that let the light in*', to live in awe and love for every cell in our natural system so that the cells change the system rather than having the system change the cells. The alternative is simply not an option. *"We'll we all shine on … Like the moon and the stars and the sun."* Instant Karma (We All Shine On) Lennon/Ono with The Plastic Ono Band, written by: John Lennon

# Section E: "Earthrise" by Amanda Gorman

## "Our Purpose in Poetry: Or, Earthrise"

### By Amanda Gorman

Dedicated to Al Gore & The Climate Reality Project

On Christmas Eve, 1968, astronaut Bill Anders
Snapped a photo of the Earth
As Apollo 8 orbited the Moon.
Those three guys
Were surprised
To see from their eyes
Our planet looked like an earthrise
A blue orb hovering over the Moon's gray horizon,
with deep oceans and silver skies.

It was our world's first glance at itself
Our first chance to see a shared reality,
A declared stance and a commonality;

A glimpse into our planet's mirror,
And as threats drew nearer,
Our own urgency became clearer,

As we realize that we hold nothing dearer
than this floating body we all call home.

We've known
That we're caught in the throes
Of climactic changes some say
Will just go away,
While some simply pray
To survive another day;
For it is the obscure, the oppressed, the poor,
Who when the disaster
Is declared done,
Still suffer more than anyone.

We refuse to lose.
Together we do this and more
Not because it's very easy or nice
But because it is necessary,
Because with every dawn we carry
the weight of the fate of this celestial body orbiting a star.
And as heavy as that weight sounded, it doesn't hold us down,
But it keeps us grounded, steady, ready,
Because an environmental movement of this size
Is simply another form of an earthrise.

To see it, close your eyes.
Visualize that all of us leaders in this room
and outside of these walls or in the halls, all
of us changemakers are in a spacecraft,
Floating like a silver raft

in space, and we see the face of our planet anew.

We relish the view;

We witness its round green and brilliant blue,

Which inspires us to ask deeply, wholly:

What can we do?

Open your eyes.

Know that the future of

this wise planet

Lies right in sight:

Right in all of us. Trust

this earth uprising.

All of us bring light to exciting solutions never tried before

For it is our hope that implores us, at our uncompromising core,

To keep rising up for an Earth more than worth fighting for.

# CHAPTER 4

# ONENESS

***Expect Earthrise:***

"...Open your eyes.
Know that the future of
this wise planet
Lies right in sight:
Right in all of us. Trust
this earth uprising.
All of us bring light to exciting solutions never tried before
For it is our hope that implores us, at our uncompromising core,
To keep rising up for an Earth more than worth fighting for."

"Earthrise" by Amanda Gorman

## The Story of Thrival

**J**ust in time there arose, as foretold in prophecies reaching back more than a thousand years, a great coming together of humanity. In the time of the Great Turning, as humans came to call it, our Wise Mother Nature—Gaia—looked upon her creation and she was disappointed.

As Gaia had with all her children, she encouraged them to explore the precious blue, green, and white planet she created for them. In her wisdom, she knew that in order for her children to thrive in the full potential of their purpose, they would need to experiment and learn from their failures and their successes. She was disappointed that the wisest of her children, Humanity, had succumbed to its own sense of invincibility and superiority. Gaia knew this was a necessary phase of development, for the rebirth of life at every stage is like Butterfly emerging from its pupa into the light of day. It was as she had designed it to be.

Gaia had been so very pleased with her child, Tree, as Tree emerged into adulthood and embodied some of Mother's most important wisdoms, among them: power-*with* is greater than power-*over*; the whole is the part, and the part is the whole. Tree, with Gaia's guidance, had learned to grow, to communicate, to sustain its brothers and sisters, and Tree thrived in great forests, living long, and lending great strength and vitality to her creation.

So, Gaia, as is her manner, dropped the pebbles of her wisdom into the spirit of the adolescent Human. She had hoped that her special child would appreciate her design and co-evolve with less supervision. She had hoped that Tree's example might be enough to guide her self-absorbed child. She worried that she had placed too much confidence in her crowning achievement as Human grew ever more selfish and separate.

In her wisdom, She placed pebbles containing her great wisdom. She chose the pebbles purposefully, knowing they would grow into beautiful Pearls of Wisdom that would guide and please her still young and developing child.

Gaia knew that the Deep Divers would be the first to find the pearls hidden in the envelopes of their shell hosts. The Deep Divers, as was their custom, would gather in Circle before the dive to give thanks to their Mother and to center their compassion for her creation. They would collect the oysters and carry them out of the darkness of the deep sea toward the light. They gathered around their harvest on the beach to crack the shells. The cracks let the light in to reveal the pearls, which they plucked out and polished. In the full light of day, the lining of each shell and every pearl shone in a glorious rainbow of colors befitting their encoded messages. The divers knew that their work was good, and they gave Gaia thanks.

Wise Mother Gaia knew that her teenage Human would value Pearl, so she endowed each Pearl of Wisdom with the power to turn that value into Mother Gaia's shared values through the messages she sent. But, her adolescent offspring, in the faint dawn-light of their existence, still could not clearly read Pearl's wisdom messages.

Thus, like Gaia had done for her other children and for beloved Tree, she composed a message written in broad strokes across the sky for the benefit of all Creation and especially for her self-absorbed children.

The message told them that the greatest value of all flows from the customs and practices that generate the greatest values for the whole of creation: **Caretakers Unite For the Good of All, NOW!**

And so, it came to be that Human emerged like Butterfly and started to flap its wings, and the fluctuations of the butterfly's wings spread out in ever-widening circles to unite with the ripples of the Pearls of Wisdom, coming together as a great wave of light to restore the essential harmony and balance of Gaia's creation.

Grateful for Mother Gaia's gift of survival, Humans rang the bells and named the new era: "Thrival."

May We All Rise in Oneness For the Good of All, NOW!

www.forthegoodofallnow.org

Made in the USA
Middletown, DE
28 October 2022

13630392R00095